MW00967145

EDISTO RIVER COMPANION

By Ken Driggers

Sponsored by

MeadWestvaco

PALMETTO CONSERVATION

Palmetto Conservation Foundation/PCF Press
With Photography by Bill Price
2008

Published in Columbia, South Carolina by:
Palmetto Conservation Foundation/PCF Press
1314 Lincoln Street, Suite 305
Columbia, SC 29201
www.palmettoconservation.org

10 9 8 7 6 5 4 3 2

Copyright 2008 Palmetto Conservation Foundation
All rights reserved.

Author: Kenneth Driggers
Editor: Virginia Ravenel
Research: Adam McConnoughy, Suzette Anderson
Maps: Steve Collum
Design & Layout: Susan Jones Ferguson
Unless otherwise noted, all photographs by Bill Price

Printed by Service Printing, Columbia, SC

The information contained in this publication was carefully checked and rechecked for accuracy. However, the publishers and writers cannot and do not guarantee the accuracy of it. No responsibility can be, or is, assumed.

Library of Congress Cataloging-in-Publication Data

Driggers, Ken, 1959-
  The Edisto River companion / Ken Driggers ; with photography by Bill
Price ; sponsored by MeadWestvaco.
     p. cm.
  ISBN-13: 978-0-9745284-8-9 (pbk.)
  1. Edisto River (S.C.)--Description and travel. 2. Edisto River Region
(S.C.)--Description and travel. 3. Edisto River Watershed
(S.C.)--Description and travel. 4. Natural history--South
Carolina--Edisto River Region. 5. Edisto River (S.C.)--Pictorial works.
6. Edisto River Region (S.C.)--Pictorial works. 7. Edisto River Region
(S.C.)--Guidebooks. I. Price, Bill, 1956- II. MeadWestvaco (Firm) III.
Palmetto Conservation Foundation. IV. Title.
  F277.E25D75 2008
  917.57'9--dc22
                        2008002462

Opposite Page:The colors of the Edisto can appeal to visitors throughout the year.

Table of Contents

    The River's Course
    The History of the Edisto River Basin
    A Historic Landscape
    Wetlands: In Between Water and Land
    An Abundance of Wildlife
    Small Town South Carolina
    Recreation for Everyone

Foreward

MeadWestvaco is proud to partner with the Palmetto Conservation Foundation to share the secrets of this ancient blackwater that winds from the Midlands to the sea. We hope you and your family will enjoy the *Edisto River Companion* guide and use it to explore the ever-changing faces and easy graces of the Edisto.

South Carolinians take great pride in the land—hiking the forests, fishing the creeks, paddling the rivers and marshes. These traditions are passed through the generations and bind us all in our love of the land.

Our employees live and work here and care deeply about the unique character of our communities. The Edisto is a part of our shared heritage as is the land that sustains us. During our decades of ownership, we've studied every aspect of this land from the soils and the plant and animal life it supports to the historic and cultural legacies of those who've come before us.

Our commitment to stewardship is central to everything we do. Protecting the natural beauty and preserving the water quality of the Edisto River is an important part of that commitment. MeadWestvaco has placed a conservation easement on the majority of our land bordering the Edisto River. And our forests are managed to internationally recognized forest certification standards, ensuring that while we grow and harvest trees for products, we are doing our part to protect special areas.

We are committed to protecting this special resource and hope you will enjoy and appreciate the Edisto as much as we do.

Kenneth T. Seeger
Senior Vice President, MeadWestvaco

MeadWestvaco

The Edisto River

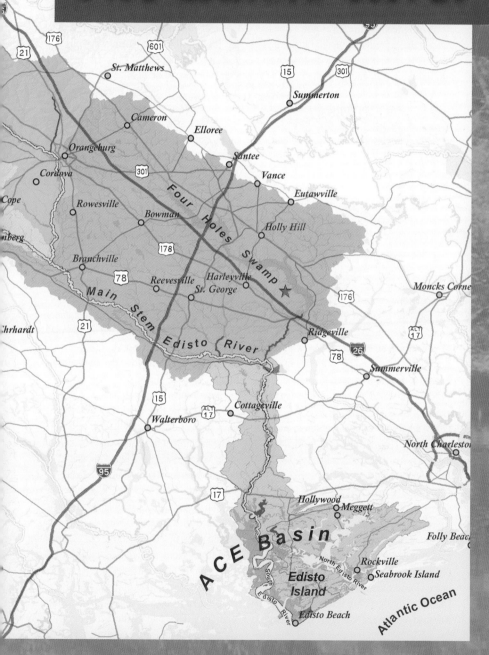

Introduction

National *Geographic Adventure Magazine* has named the Edisto River one of the top 50 amazing places in North America.[1] As the River flows slowly through the cypress and tupelo forests, it is easy to see why. It is even easier to wonder how anything could outplace the Edisto.

The Edisto is described as a blackwater river. Technically this means the water that flows from the cypress swamps yields tannin acids. These acids, mixed with decaying leaves and sand, give the River a dark look. Looks can be deceiving. The water is usually so clear you can see the bottom. This is the Edisto's special quality. It looks black, but at a closer look, it is like looking at a glass of tea in the light.

Blackwater rivers have another claim to fame. They are some of the cleanest natural waters in the world. The acidic, almost sterile water keeps bacteria under control. This is one of the reasons the waters of the Edisto are so pure.

And yet, an additional fact worth mentioning is that no dams exist on the Edisto. It missed the era of great dam building that changed the course of many of South Carolina's great rivers. The Edisto's natural features worked to its advantage. The swampy land throughout the Basin makes the River hard to dam. The water would back up forever.

Some people claim the Edisto is the longest, free-flowing blackwater river in North America. It is, after all, 250 miles long. While its place as the champion river can be argued, most people agree that the Edisto is one of the few remaining blackwater river systems in the United States in good ecological shape. Undisputedly, the Edisto is a free-flowing, un-dammed, ecologically-healthy river running through a great portion of South Carolina. This alone should attract your attention.

While traveling in most communities in South Carolina, you'll notice references to the term Edisto. Streets and restaurants take the name to connect to a wonderful part of the South Carolina experience. What is the special place that these labels refer to?

The source of all this wonder is the Edisto River. The Edisto is the only river system entirely within the borders of the state. It starts in the Midlands and ends at the Atlantic Ocean, traversing a number of ecosystems. There is much to see along the way, and the sites are as diverse as is South Carolina. The Edisto River Basin supports 94 ecological communities, including threatened and endangered species. Animals thrive around the River. The State Department of Natural Resources claims that 87 freshwater species and 120 saltwater species of fish have been collected from the Edisto.[2]

There is also much history along the banks of the Edisto. From the old plantation economy along the coast to the agricultural heartland at the River's headwaters, there are glimpses of the culture that built today's South Carolina. Throw in the depression-era architecture decorating many of South Carolina's state parks, and, in a few short days on the Edisto, you will have a good understanding of the state's past and present.

Many people have found out that the Edisto River is something to see and something to experience. It is probably South Carolina's second most popular recreational river after the Upstate's Chattooga. During certain times of the year, traffic can get down-right heavy along parts of it. But there is still a quiet spot for those who seek it.

The Edisto River portrays South Carolina in its natural splendor and cultural traditions. The state's history and beauty are present there for the seeking. Come be a companion on the journey.

8

1. Mark Kirby, "Carolina Road Trip, Friends in Low Places," *National Geographic Adventure Magazine*, March 2006.
2. SC Department of Natural Resources (Edisto River Task Force), "Managing Resources for a Sustainable Future, *The Edisto River Basin Project Report*," 1996, p.126.

Before Heading Out on the Edisto River

10 Outdoor Trip Essentials [3]

Aday spent enjoying the Edisto can be a fun experience for the entire family. But outdoor adventure also poses risks. To avoid problems, remember to carry along these outdoor trip essentials.

1. Adequate water and food
2. Trail or topographic map
3. Compass
4. Adequate clothing (including rain gear and sunglasses)
5. Knife
6. First-aid kit
7. Headlamp or flashlight
8. Waterproof matches
9. Signaling device (whistle or mirror)
10. Insect repellent

Leave No Trace [4]

The Edisto River is one of South Carolina's greatest natural wonders. It should be enjoyed *and* respected by all who use it. Please remember to practice the "Leave No Trace" rules when visiting the Edisto River.

• Plan ahead and prepare: know regulations and concerns of the area before you visit. Prepare for weather and other potential hazards.

• Travel and camp on durable surfaces: use established trails and campsites. Consider your impact on the environment around you at all times.

• Dispose of waste properly: pack it in; pack it out.

• Leave what you find: preserve the past and all natural objects.

• Minimize campfire impacts: keep fires small and use established rings or pans.

• Respect wildlife: observe from a distance and never feed animals.

• Be considerate of other visitors: respect others and add to the quality of their experience.

Visit www.lnt.org for more information.

Photo courtesy of Bill Marshall and FRED.

Group floats down the Edisto are a popular activity.

3. *The Catawba River Companion*, (Columbia, SC: PCF Press, 203), p. 28.
4. The Center for Outdoor Ethics, "*Leave No Trace*," August 24, 2007, (http://www/lnt.org).

How to Get There by Car

Not everyone is lucky enough to see the Edisto River from the water. For most of us, traveling by automobile will be how we view the scenery of the region. Fortunately, there are many great routes that traverse the Basin that will allow the adventurous traveler to get off the interstate and really experience South Carolina culture. To see a wide swath of the Basin, you will need to cut back-and-forth across the River. Take a look at the overview map to plan your visit.

Here are some routes to keep in mind:

US Highways 78, 178, and **301** are major asphalt tributaries that take you from the Midlands to the Lowcountry.

US Highways 1, 321, and **17** form a nice matrix that allows a good cross-matrix of communities.

Of course, you can take **Interstates 95** and **26** and get there faster. But think of what you will miss.

Many roads to Edisto Beach, like this one, are lined with majestic oaks.

How to Use this Guide

disto River Companion is a guide for people to enjoy the Edisto River. It is a history book, a travel book, and a celebration of the attractions, places, and people that make the Edisto River Basin such a great place to visit. One in a series of PCF's guides featuring South Carolina's great rivers, the *Edisto River Companion* is not intended to be an all-encompassing resource, but it is a great place to start planning a trip.

We suggest you begin by turning to the overview map and the section called "Understanding the Edisto." This will give you a feel for the River's course as well as its history and natural environment. Then we feature four sections of the River: the North Fork, the South Fork, the Main Stem and Four Holes Swamp, and the ACE Basin and Edisto Island. As you look through the overview map, if you notice something that interests you, just flip to that section for more details.

Each of the four sections opens with a colorful **map** that contains **access points** where you can get on and off the River. They are listed on the map as boat ramps. The name of the ramp is listed in a highlighted box. Following each map is detailed information about places to see and things to do within that area. We include highlights called Day Trips, Destinations, and Interesting Facts in each section.

Destinations are the key cities near the River. An icon signifies Destinations and looks like this:

Day Trips are local places where visitors can while away a few hours. These are usually popular sites, such as wilderness areas and parks, but they might also include visitor centers or botanical gardens. An icon signifies Day Trips and looks like this:

Interesting Facts are nestled among the different destinations in each section. These unusual aspects of a section of the River reveal something that makes the Edisto special. Sometimes they involve history, sometimes they involve nature. Interesting Facts appear in the sidebars on a page.

At the end of each section is a list of more attractions to visit in that area. Museums, parks, and other points of interest are included here to allow you to design a visit according to your particular interest.

The Edisto River is immense in scope and grandeur. The *Edisto River Companion* points you in the right direction and points out others who can help you see the Edisto. While this information is a good start, don't exclude other places along the River that could be more to your liking and could add a special flavor to your trip. Take advantage of the many sources of information that can help you find the right way to enjoy your time along the Edisto.

Understanding the Edisto

The Edisto River Basin is a diverse part of South Carolina. The watershed represents a 12-county area that contains 3,120 square miles. In 1996, the South Carolina Department of Natural Resources studied the Edisto; it took over 200 citizens to form a cross section of the region to represent the various interests with a stake in the River's future.

The River's Course

The Edisto begins in the Midlands. Its tributaries rise out of swamps in Aiken, Edgefield, Lexington, and Saluda Counties. The two northern branches, the South and North Forks, begin here. The North Fork begins in Lexington County, the South Fork in Edgefield. Both Forks are tiny, quick-moving streams. Paddlers think the North Fork, in particular, can be a challenge to navigate because of the tight corridor and rapid currents.

The two Forks converge near the Orangeburg-Bamberg county line, creating the Main Stem. Here, where the Forks come together, the River slows down. Nature lovers can sense a transition from hardwoods to tupelo.

The well-known Edisto River Canoe and Kayak Trail is a 56-mile trail on the River's Main Stem. The sandbars created by the slow waters have led to a tradition. Regular paddlers use the sandbars as a resting place. The especially hearty outdoorsman uses them for overnight camping.

Also along the Main Stem is Four Holes Swamp, known by many people as the home of Beidler Forest. Here, the Edisto is not really a river, but a collection of springs that form a swamp. If you want to see what a real swamp is like, this is the place to visit.

Finally, the Main Stem gives way to the ACE Basin and Edisto Island. There are 12,000 acres of rice fields around the tidal areas. When you get to the end, you have arrived at South Carolina's coast, one of the country's premiere vacation destinations.

The River ends at Edisto Beach. By following the River from beginning to end, you can experience the transition of South Carolina from coastal plain to coastal edge. If your starting point was the River's headwaters, you have traveled 250 miles to the Atlantic Ocean, and you have also traversed the longest and largest river system completely inside South Carolina's borders.

The History of the Edisto River Basin

It is hard to separate the River from its history. The slow-moving River encompasses a lot of South Carolina and its history. Most of the region is still undeveloped, and a lot of its history is still part of the local fabric. Change can come slowly in this part of South Carolina.

The Edisto, like many other places in South Carolina, is an Indian name. The original inhabitants of the area were Native Americans. Historical accounts indicate there were numerous tribes in the South Carolina Lowcountry.

There is record of a Cusabo tribe called Edisto that lived near the lower Edisto River and eventually on Edisto Island. Relations between the Edisto Indians and early settlers were often strained. In 1674, the Earl of Shaftsbury, a powerful Lord's Proprietor, bought Edisto Island from the Indians, and what was left of the tribe, by then, was probably pushed inland. Between disease and the constant war among various Indian tribes, the original Edisto Indians and other coastal tribes were decimated. The few survivors probably joined with other Indians whose tribes had suffered the same fate. Many tribal distinctions were probably lost; the original Edisto tribe was no more.

What we know today as the Edisto Indians is a combination of two tribes: the Kusso and the Natchez. The Kusso are recorded by Spanish explorers to have lived in the Edisto River area further inland as early as 1577. They were farmers, fishermen, and hunters. The Natchez Indians came to South Carolina from the Mississippi Valley where they were ousted from their land. One small group of survivors came to settle in South Carolina in Four Holes Swamp around 1735, where they lived until 1744.

Eventually the two tribes joined together and continued to live around the Edisto River from the mid-1700s to the present. Today they live in the Four Holes area of Dorchester County and in the Creeltown area of Colleton County. Though they are the Kusso-Natchez Indians, they have long been called Edisto Indians. To avoid confusion over the name, the tribe elected to officially adopt the name Edisto in 1975.[5] The tribe holds an annual powwow to preserve and share the tribe's heritage, history, and culture.

Once a successful colony was established in 1670 in Charlestowne, other Europeans made their way to South Carolina. English, Scotch-Irish, German, Swiss, and French immigrants came in search of a better life and the promise of land. Many of their descendants still live

The Edisto Needs Friends

Everything needs to be loved. For the Edisto River, this role belongs to a special friend called FRED.

Friends of the Edisto, or FRED, is a volunteer group that loves the River. The group has adopted a mission "to protect and enhance the natural and cultural character and resources of the Edisto River Basin through conservation and responsible use." Their members pursue this mission through education, research, and advocacy. Most importantly, as the local paper put it, "The people of FRED are more than talk; the people with FRED put their feet on the River's banks."

If you, too, want to be a Friend of the Edisto, visit its Web site at www.edistofriends.org. You will find tons of information on the River and how to enjoy it. Better yet, use the Web site to become a member. If you love a friend, you need to support it.

in the small towns along the Edisto River Basin. As the population increased in the coastal areas, these settlers began moving inland using the navigable Edisto River and numerous Indian trails that existed. They built towns around the trading posts already established as a result of the fur trade.

There were many dangers for these

5. Herb McAmis, *Indian People of the Edisto River,* (Ridgeville, SC: Four Holes Indian Association and Edisto Indian Council), p. 5.

The Edisto River Basin has many cypress forests.

early settlers. Indian attacks, wild animals, and disease threatened the survival of those who moved inland. Despite the threats, the land held much promise for those who were industrious. It was a fertile land with great natural resources. Agriculture has been a leading industry in the Edisto River Basin since the early days. Corn grew well in the fertile soil and kept many settlers alive during the early years of hardship.

The land was also rich in timber. It was covered in yellow pine and cypress trees. Lumbering began in the early years of settlement and has continued to be an important resource even today. Eventually the industrious settlers created a new industry around the production of resin, tar, pitch, and turpentine. Cypress wood was popular because it was so durable and termite resistant. The River offered a natural source of power for the many sawmills and grist mills that sprang up.

By the early 1700s, rice planting in the coastal zone was the leading crop of South Carolina and continued to be an important source of income on and off for the next 150 years. Huge rice plantations were built up and down the Edisto River near the coast in the tidal river swamplands. Nearly 12,000 acres where "Carolina Gold" rice once grew are evident along the Edisto River system. Today most of these plantations are maintained as waterfowl habitats. When rice prices fell, the farmers looked for other cash crops to plant. They discovered indigo grew well in the area, so it became an important source of income for both Lowcountry planters and small inland farmers until the American Revolution.

The struggle for American Independence played a large role in the region's history. Several Revolutionary War events took place in the Edisto Basin. The state legislature met in the town of Jacksonboro in 1782, while Charleston was occupied by the British. The Revolutionary War Battle of Parker's Ferry took place on the Edisto River in 1781. During his southern tour, President George Washington crossed the Edisto near Jacksonboro. Today much of the River has the same character as when President Washington saw it.

In the 1800s, the road systems

14

were still inferior along the Edisto River Basin. Farmers and loggers used the River to transport crops and felled trees. This early industry helped spark a need for better transportation. Improved road ways, bridges, and the railroad resulted. The first South Carolina railroad project began in 1830 and was completed in 1833 from Charleston to Hamburg. Towns like Blackville and Branchville grew rapidly, and the railroad enabled farmers to get their produce to market quicker.

The Civil War and Sherman's march through South Carolina devastated most of this area. Fields lay idle, and many homes and businesses were pillaged and burned, which left residents homeless and penniless. Some large plantations were sold into smaller tracts. Farmers struggled

Gullah - A Unique Culture

The large concentration of Africans in the old plantation economy in the lower part of the Basin has left a noticeable and unique culture called Gullah. Among the Gullah, African traits continued in culinary practices, folklore, song, and language. In recent years, the Gullah people have struggled to preserve their traditional culture. Many visitors to the region notice Gullah basket weavers selling their wares along Lowcountry roads. Basket making is one of the most visible Gullah practices today.

to pay the taxes on their land. This period marked a renaissance for Lowcountry plantations as their use changed from farming to hunting. It took years to recover, but recovery came and many farmers planted cotton. Cotton became the leading cash crop, which earned it the name "King Cotton."

Cotton remained king until the boll weevil came in the 1920s. The farmers along the Edisto River Basin had to diversify. Many turned to planting peanuts, and others started growing truck crops.

The rich soil along the Edisto River Basin was ideal for growing cucumbers, melons, cantaloupes, strawberries, and cabbage. Dairy production increased, and the timber industry remained strong.

The cotton era ended by the 1950s. As factories were built across the state, the great majority of farmers left agriculture. The rural landscape remains in much of the Edisto Basin, reminding current visitors of the traditional industries along the Edisto River.

The ACE Basin is a key part of the area. It is also a region where natural beauty reigns supreme. Many of the large plantations that once supplied the mills with timber were converted to hunting preserves. The abandoned rice fields and logged forests attracted a rich abundance of game animals, including migratory waterfowl and deer. Several governmental and nonprofit partners began the ACE Basin Project in the 1980s to protect these properties from commercial exploitation. The ACE Basin Project has received national recognition for its success in protecting significant areas.

In 1970, when South Carolina celebrated its Tricentennial, more than 80 percent of its residents had been born in the state. Since then, however, South Carolina's natural beauty and beaches have been discovered. The Edisto Basin, particularly the coastal areas but increasingly inland as well, has become more popular as a tourist destination and a magnet for new arrivals.

At the bottom of the Basin, Edisto Beach is an attractive tourist destination. It is becoming more popular for year-round residents. Development began in the 1920s, when beachgoers would visit the beach, timing their arrival to coincide with low tide so that they could cross the marsh areas by driving on beds of oyster shells. Development was slow in the early days. Damage from a hurricane in 1940 destroyed many of the existing homes. Following World War II, development began to increase. South Carolina's tourism economy was beginning to come alive, and Edisto Beach joined the movement.

One of the main north-south highways, US 301, bisects the region. Long before the interstate system, Highway 301 served as a major artery for people heading south. At that time, before I-95, Highway 301 was the most traveled route from New York to Florida. Today commercial establishments that used to be major stops on a north-south journey still serve as reminders of a different age.

With the completion of I-95, travelers gained speed; some locations became forgotten. Today these "lost places" still reveal the interchange between people, cultures, and experiences. According to the US Census Bureau, only five counties along this route of interstate are completely rural. Two of these are in South Carolina.

History has been grand along the Edisto. Fortunately for those who love the area's rural splendor, this history remains a key part of the Edisto experience.

A Historic Landscape

When you travel across the Edisto Basin, you will see historic changes in the landscape. On the North and South Forks of the River, the architecture shows the small farming customary to the Ridge and Midlands of South Carolina. Traditional Upstate farm houses dot the roadways in Lexington and Orangeburg Counties. Occasionally, a true gem of a historic house will reveal itself to a traveler. It is not uncommon to see a sign designating a site as a Bicentennial Farm, one that has been in agriculture for over 200 years.

In the lower reaches of the Basin, along the River's Main Stem and into the coastal area, evidence of the great plantation culture emerges. The plantation culture that was part of the founding of South Carolina and the United States was situated in this part of the Edisto Basin. Numerous plantation homes still exist that are grand in scale and in tradition. Periodic plantation tours are offered by the historical societies in Colleton and Beaufort Counties. They are well worth the visit.

At the coast, the landscape turns to recreation. Edisto Beach is a great part of the booming vacation economy of coastal South Carolina. Well known for its laid-back lifestyle, Edisto Beach is a good place to see what has made South Carolina among the country's premiere vacation destinations.

Wetlands: In Between Water and Land

To the casual observer, the Edisto River Basin may be a swampy area filled with exotic creatures and plants but to the

Historic churches, like this one in Walterboro, give a glimpse of the past.

16

White Ibis landing on the Edisto River.

ecologist, the Edisto River Basin is among the most diverse places to be found. It is a wetlands paradise.

Wetlands are places where water is present a great deal of the time. Sometimes a wetland is defined by the presence of wetlands soil, sometimes by the vegetation and fauna found there. No matter how you define it, the Edisto River Basin is among the most wetlands-diverse spots in America. The South Carolina Department of Natural Resources estimates there are 683,390 acres of wetlands within the Edisto Basin.[6] They play a wide range of important ecological roles.

The wetlands along the Edisto take various forms. Most are associated with the River and take their direction from the River's flow. In the upper sections along the North and South Forks, wetlands are found in the narrow floodplains. Near Orangeburg and along the Main Stem, you can observe pine flatwoods where the area is poorly drained. Further south along the coast, the influence of marshlands gives the area a distinctive Lowcountry feel.

Keep an eye out for Carolina Bays, which can be found throughout the Basin. These isolated wetlands are usually elliptical and resemble giant paw prints in the soil. They continue to raise curiosity because of their diverse habitats and the uncertainty of their origin. They are a truly special part of South Carolina.

River Politics

It has been an unusual path into politics for Charlie Sweat. He has gone from conservationist to town father.

Charlie helped to organize the immensely popular Edisto River Canoe and Kayak Trail. He was then elected mayor of Walterboro. From this vantage point, he understands what the Edisto River means to his community.

"SC PR&T was trying to figure out how to help promote rural state parks. Our two—Colleton State Park and Givhans Ferry State Park—had the River in common, so they decided to promote their parks by promoting the River."

A group of volunteers put together the first Edisto Riverfest. This festival takes place the second weekend in June, which is National Rivers Month. They recruited Charlie to help with the logistics. As he put it, "The Edisto had the reputation as the easiest river in SC to 'drown on.' We received a $10,000 county accommodations tax grant to purchase boats and paddles. All this success for a public investment of $10,000. There's a lesson in that."

What attracted Charlie to the River? He claims it is "the peace and quiet of the River . . . the beauty that is out there. I grew up here and have gone on the Edisto all my life. But like most people, I had never really experienced the River."

The Edisto has grown to be a large part of the Walterboro community and Charlie's life. Sweat explains, "From a conservationist's standpoint, the Trail's popularity is a good thing. People who make their living off the Edisto realize that the quality of their business depends on the quality of the River. From a personal standpoint, the success has helped my political career. I have met people from around the state who help Walterboro."

17

SC Department of Natural Resources (Edisto River Basin Task Force), "Managing Resources for A Sustainable Future, *The Edisto River Basin Report,*" October 1996, p.126.

Birdwatchers might see a Tufted Titmouse along the Edisto River Basin.

An Abundance of Wildlife

The bottomland forest and prime agricultural fields in the Edisto Basin are home to an abundance of wildlife that makes the region one of the richest habitats in the southeast. The "Edisto River Basin Report" found that 45 percent of the Basin remains in land uses that represent natural habitats.[7] This continued, traditional use of the land means good things for visitors who are looking to experience the wildlife of the area. White tail deer and the eastern wild turkey live here.

A trip to the Edisto would not seem right without sighting an alligator. In warmer months, it is quite common to see one cruising along. Don't panic. They are probably more afraid of you than you are of them.

The Edisto Basin is home to several threatened or significant species, including the red-cockaded woodpecker, southern bald eagle, wood stork, loggerhead turtle, and short nosed sturgeon. These species find the undisturbed forest and habitat along the River to their liking.

Recreational fishermen find the 250 miles of river on the Edisto to be an alluring attraction. Good water quality and undisturbed buffers make the River a rich habitat for 189 fish species. The redbreast sunfish, striped bass, and the American shad are particularly important part of the ecosystem. The flathead catfish, though not indigenous to the River, can also be found. And, remember, the Edisto leads into the Atlantic Ocean, where the saltwater species are too numerous to list.

For the birdwatcher, the Edisto Basin is paradise. During the fall and winter, eagles and waterfowl are common. Orangeburg's Edisto Gardens is a good spot to visit because it is home to all types of upland birds, birds of prey, waterfowl, wading birds, and songbirds. Beidler Forest, which hosts the annual Christmas Bird Count, is part of the largest private reserve for red-cockaded woodpecker habitat in North America.

No mention of birding would be complete without a note about the ACE Basin. This spectacular wetlands wilderness offers several good spots to see several different species. The old rice fields attract waterfowl by the droves and make for some interesting afternoons of exploration.

A white tailed buck drinking from the River's edge.

Small Town South Carolina

The Edisto River Basin is a region of great small towns. The largest town, Aiken, is home to approximately 25,000 people. Orangeburg on the North Fork and Walterboro on the Main Stem boast 13,000 and 5,500 citizens respectively. Clearly big-city life is

7. National Audubon Society, The Francis Beidler Forest in Four Holes Swamp, *A Self Guided Tour Of The Boardwalk*, 1978, p. 3.

not to be found along the Edisto River.

What can be found are dozens of unique and charming small communities. Visit Johnston on the South Fork or North on the North Fork and you can capture a glimpse of how life has always been in these traditional farming communities. Further toward the River, a coastal influence takes over. While you may find more traffic, you continue to experience the smiling faces and long-time traditions of South Carolina's small towns. If you want to truly learn what life along the Edisto is like, spend some time in one of these communities. A few hours living among the locals can result in a new appreciation for rural South Carolina.

Recreation for Everyone

The Edisto is a recreational river. A wide variety of outdoor pursuits can be enjoyed along the Basin. There is no wonder that the Edisto is now considered one of South Carolina's premiere tourism resources and is often included in the advertising to out-of-state visitors.

Hunters find the farm fields along the northern stretches of the River superb habitat for game animals. The plantations

Photo courtesy of Bill Marshall

of the ACE Basin remain undeveloped because owners protect them for their hunting potential.

Of course fishermen love the Edisto. During the American Revolution, British General Lord Cornwallis loved it so much that he wrote that saving the colonies was worth the effort just for the redbreast sunfish. Fishermen today would agree.

Recreational boating is a huge pursuit up and down the River. Along the coast, power boats are a way of life. The 56-mile Edisto Canoe and Kayak Trail continues to attract more users each year.

Do not forget simple "beach loving." At the bottom of the River, Edisto Beach attracts thousands each year as families return to enjoy the laid-back atmosphere of one of South Carolina's great destinations.

He Knows Rivers: Barry Beasley

Columbian Barry Beasley knows rivers. For years, he was director of the South Carolina Scenic River program, acquiring a national reputation as an expert on and protector of rivers. He is South Carolina's leading expert on rivers and today directs all land protection programs for the state's Department of Natural Resources. He is co-author of the popular book *The Rivers of South Carolina*.

Beasley claims the Edisto River, for all its natural splendor, is probably more important to South Carolina culturally. "There has been a strong attachment to the River for a long time. The Edisto has an aura about it . . . It has an intimacy that draws people to it."

According to Beasley, a trip down the Edisto changes a person's perspective. "A trip down the Edisto changes people's perceptions as to what a swamp is. They are normally accustomed to the marshland wetlands of the Lowcountry, but the clear water of the Edisto is an utterly different experience."

"I was asked to lead an outing for the National Sierra Club in the early 1980s," says Beasley. "I put together a four-day trip for a group from across the nation who was as familiar as anyone with the scope and beauty of our country's natural resources. I was worried about meeting their expectations. The Edisto didn't fail. I remember a female Sierra Club leader from the Chicago area was especially impressed. She said, 'The Edisto weaves a spell. I will never look at rivers the same way because of the Edisto.'"

19

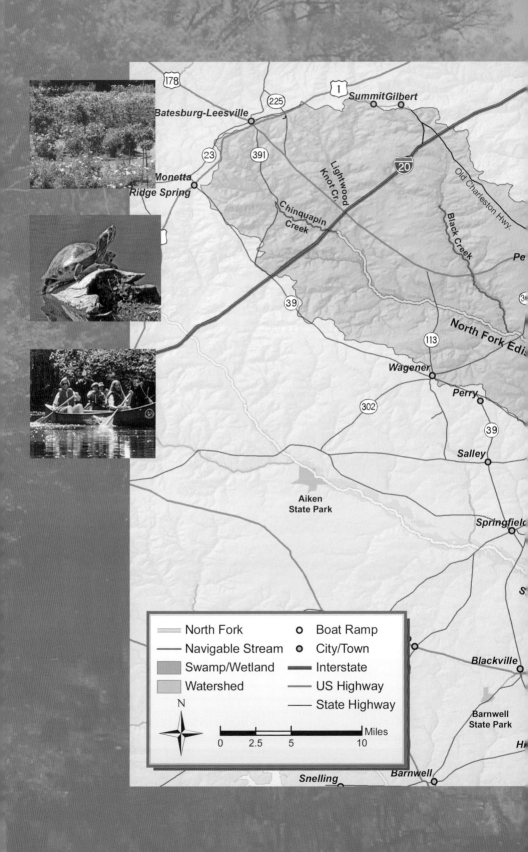

178

225

1   Summit Gilbert

Batesburg-Leesville

23   391

Lightwood Knot Cr.

20

Old Charleston Hwy.

Monetta
Ridge Spring

Chinquapin
Creek

Black Creek

Pe

39

North Fork Edis

113

Wagener

Perry

302

39

Salley

Aiken
State Park

Springfield

North Fork

Navigable Stream

Swamp/Wetland

Watershed

N

Boat Ramp

City/Town

Interstate

US Highway

State Highway

Miles

0   2.5   5   10

Blackville

Barnwell
State Park

S

H

Snelling   Barnwell

The North Fork

o f   t h e   E d i s t o   R i v e r

Cayce

th Congaree
302

321

Gaston

Congaree
National Park

Congaree River

Swansea
6

692

21

176

Woodford

172

6 St. Matthews

Pooles Mill

Bull Swamp Creek

North

Jones Bridge

601

Carson Park

Slab

389 Livingston

Cameron

Neeses

Baughman

Caw Caw Swamp

4

Slab Landing Road

Shillings Bridge Rd.

321

400

Orangeburg

33

Orangeburg 301

Norway

Cordova

178

332

601

21

Cannon Brdg. Rd.

Livingston

301

Pou's

Rowesville

Cope

Rowe's Bridge

o River

78

Denmark

Bamberg

Kill Kare

Branchville

When traveling through the territory . . .

. . . around the Edisto's North Fork, it is important to remember how the area was founded. Fertile soils made it an attractive place to settle. The River provided a connection to many communities, both big and small, to share crops and commerce. The Swiss, German, and Dutch immigrants that settled here formed a small community near the banks of the North Edisto River. The town that became Orangeburg soon was a well-established hub on the North Fork, and so it remains today.

Located just beyond the sprawling Columbia metropolitan area, the upper reaches of the North Fork lie on "The Ridge," a geographic feature often used in the names of businesses and community groups. The Ridge is a dividing point for more than simple geography; it is also where Columbia stops and rural living begins. The small town of North can be considered the mid-point of the North Fork. For those who want to see the River up close and personal, getting on or off at North is key.

Orangeburg is the southern focal point of the North Fork, so to speak. For a city its size, it is surprisingly sophisticated. It is a perfect place to get off the River, especially when you leave your boat in the middle of the Edisto Memorial Gardens, one of the most picturesque spots in South Carolina. Make sure you leave time to smell the roses; there are plenty of them.

The small towns on The Ridge have a lot in common and probably share a lot with small towns across America. Historic main streets, historic homes, and smiling faces fill the towns of Swansea, Gilbert, Ridge Springs, and Monetta. Wander from one community to the next, and you see that farming is still a way of life along The Ridge. Scenic cotton and soybean fields line the roads.

DESTINATION:
The Ridge

Drive down US Highway 178, and you notice countless references to The Ridge. Look at a geographic map of South Carolina, and you will see why. The Ridge is that hilly section of the state lying in Lexington, Saluda, and Aiken Counties. It is a fertile plateau about 30 miles long between clay hills to the north and sand hills to the south. Cold air seeks the lowest point, and the Ridge provides good drainage for the air that seeps into the

I n t e r e s t i n g   F a c t

Peaches and The Ridge

Peach farming came to The Ridge as an alternative crop. After the boll weevil took a bite out of the cotton industry, asparagus and peaches became its cash crops. Once South Carolina was squeezed out of the asparagus market, The Ridge depended on peaches. At one time, those living along The Ridge considered peach season a "sort of Christmas" because most of the area's economic activity took place at that time.

valleys on either side.

People in South Carolina make a distinction between the Upstate and the Lowcountry. Usually this is a cultural difference. Geographically speaking, The Ridge is what separates the two regions. Situated about 140 miles from the coast, The Ridge is at higher elevations than surrounding areas. It is covered with fertile soils that make for good farming. It's no wonder that South Carolina's Ridge produces not only a large amount of, but also some of the tastiest, peaches in the world.

DAY TRIP:
The Hidden North Fork: *The North Fork Canoe and Kayak Trail*

Many people think of the Main Stem near Walterboro when they consider experiencing the Edisto. What they don't realize is that the Edisto is a long river with many different paddling opportunities. Some paddlers say that to see the real Edisto, the North Fork is the stretch to travel. Starting at the small town of North and ending in Orangeburg, the 35-mile North Fork Canoe and Kayak Trail is narrow and winding. Without the motor boat traffic present on the more heavily traveled Main Stem Canoe and Kayak Trail, the North Fork makes for a very nice paddle.

The North Fork Canoe and Kayak Trail began through the efforts of a local nonprofit group called Friends of the Edisto. These committed river lovers built the North Fork Blueway to increase the usage along this hidden stretch of water. The Blueway's facilities have made the North Fork easier to navigate, but you still have the River to yourself. To find out more about paddling the North Fork or about FRED, visit its Web site at **www.edistofriends.org.**

DESTINATION: *Orangeburg*

The North Fork of the Edisto passes through Orangeburg, making it easy to forget you are in a city when on the River there. Travel into town, and you will find it to be a cultural destination. Orangeburg is proud to be a center of learning for South

Carolina with the campuses of South Carolina State University and Claflin College. These educational institutions add a certain youthful, college town energy to the city.

If you are interested in learning African-American history, visit the campus of South Carolina State University where many of our state's black leaders were educated. Founded in 1896 as the state's sole public college for black youth, this university has played a key role in the education of African Americans in the state and nation. A good place to start is the I.P. Stanback Museum and Planetarium, which has an impressive collection of African-American art in one of the largest exhibition areas in the state. From there you can learn about the civil rights movement and take a self-guided tour of the historical Orangeburg Cemetery where some of Orangeburg's most famous African Americans are buried.

A long day on the River can leave a person hungry. For the barbeque lover, Orangeburg is home to several renowned restaurants that feature southern-style barbeque as the main course. For lunch or dinner, barbeque in Orangeburg is worth the stop.

Photo Courtesy of Bill Marshall and FRED.

24

Edisto Memorial Gardens is a popular tourist destination in South Carolina.

DAY TRIP: *Edisto Memorial Gardens*

For the most part, a trip down the North Fork of the Edisto is an isolating river experience with little on either bank. Things change dramatically when you reach Orangeburg's Edisto Memorial Gardens. You have entered a marvelous destination on the River, right in the city of Orangeburg. Even the most wilderness-loving river rat will want to take time to enjoy this experience.

Edisto Memorial Gardens is a city-owned, 110-acre site with seasonal flowers blooming all year. There are more than 3,200 rose bushes, camellias, azaleas, and flowering trees. Some 75 labeled varieties of award-winning roses are always on display. As one of only 23 sites in the nation designated as test gardens for the All American Rose Selections, the roses here are world class.

In addition, within the Gardens lies a spectacular 2,700-foot boardwalk, the Horne Wetlands Park. The park offers a close-up look at the Edisto River's wetland ecosystem. There is so much to see, so plan to spend a good part of your day there. A restored waterwheel that was part of an old mill is especially interesting and will attract any child's attention. The park also features a boat dock with a gazebo and an interpretive shelter filled with educational materials.

For the culturally minded, the adjacent Arts Center maintains a gallery on its second floor. A beautiful terrace garden has been developed on the river side of the Arts Center. This garden also features a beautiful Centennial Park. This formal area is beautifully landscaped and features two plazas, a gazebo, and a fountain with a palmetto tree sculpture.

Don't let the natural beauty make you forget that Edisto Memorial Gardens is also a place of history. In 1865, a force of fewer than 600 Confederate soldiers gathered on

The All American roses in bloom at Edisto Memorial Gardens

the land that is now the Memorial Gardens to defend the Edisto River Bridge. These soldiers temporarily halted the advance of the Union Army.

More North Fork Attractions
Branchville Railroad Shrine and Museum

This museum is located in the oldest railroad junction in the United States. The shrine/museum teaches visitors about the Best

---

I n t e r e s t i n g   F a c t

Children's Garden Christmas

There is no better time to visit Edisto Memorial Gardens than during the winter holidays. The Children's Garden Christmas provides a lighted, one-half mile drive through the Gardens, decorated with 25 animated displays, 14 motionless displays, 60 lighted cherry trees, and a kid's walk with an additional 14 displays. The Memorial Gardens Christmas is illuminated seven days a week from the Monday before Thanksgiving through the first week of January. For a spring experience, attend the South Carolina Festival of Roses that is held the weekend before Mother's Day.

Friend of Charleston, the first railroad in the United States, which was constructed in 1833.
Location: 7204 Freedom Road, Branchville, SC (not far from where the North and South Forks meet to form the Main Stem)
Contact: Branchville Town Hall, 803-274-8820

Cooper's Creek Golf Club

Cooper's Creek Golf Club is an 18-hole professional course, requiring as much strategy as finesse.
Location: 700 Wagner Hwy, Leesville, SC
Contact: 800-828-8463

Cypress Swamp Boat Tours

Fisheagle Tours offers tours on Lake Marion that take you into cypress swamps that have become a wildlife haven since the lake was flooded during the Santee Cooper Project. Tours last about two hours.
Location: Depart from Santee State Park, Santee, SC
Contact: 803-854-4005 or 800-967-7739

Edisto Memorial Gardens

See Day Trip to Edisto Memorial Gardens on page 25.
Hours/Dates of Operation: Dawn to Dusk, Year-Round (free)
Location: 979 Middleton Street,

The Best Friend of Charleston

In the 1830s, it was the longest rail line in the world. Travel no longer depended on weather conditions. Completed in 1833, it brought prosperity to Charleston. It was the country's first railroad, the Best Friend of Charleston, a 136-mile line from Charleston to the North Fork town of Hamburg.

Today a replica housed in Charleston is the most familiar reminder of the Best Friend. In its day, the Best Friend was vital to the economies of many of the small towns along the Edisto. Their goods and products were a perfect fit for this new easy way to travel. It must have been quite a day when the Best Friend became the first locomotive to establish regular passenger service in the young and growing United States.

To get a feel for the impact of the Best Friend, visit the Railroad Shrine and Museum in the Orangeburg County town of Branchville. It is located on Highway 21 in an old railroad depot. While you visit, don't forget that Branchville calls itself the oldest railroad junction in the country.

Orangeburg, SC (off Hwy 301 South)
Contact: 800-533-6020

Elloree Heritage Museum

The Elloree Heritage Museum offers an exciting and educational view of South Carolina's rural past.
Location: 2714 Cleveland St., Elloree, SC
Contact: 803-897-2225

The I.P. Stanback Museum and Planetarium

The planetarium is located on the campus of SC State University and is SC's second largest planetarium. The museum has one of the largest exhibition areas in the state.
Hours/Dates of Operation: Planetarium programs are offered Monday-Thursday at 9, 10, and 11.

Location: SC State University, Orangeburg, SC
Contact: 803-536-7174

Lexington County Museum

The Lexington County Museum offers the opportunity to see what 18th-century southern life was really like by taking a tour of its historic buildings.
Hours/Dates of Operation: Tuesday-Saturday, 10-4; Sunday, 1-4 (last tour begins at 3 all days)
Location: 231 Fox Street at US 378, Lexington, SC
Contact: 803-359-8369

Monetta Drive-In

The "Big Mo" is an old-fashioned movie experience in the small town of Monetta.
Location: Off Historic Highway 1 (5-6 miles past Batesburg), Monetta, SC
Contact: Monetta Drive-In, 803-685-7949

Neeses Farm Museum

The Neeses Farm Museum will give you an idea of what life was like for early farmers in this area. The museum displays farm tools and equipment, ranging from butter churns to cotton gins.
Location: 6449 Savannah Hwy, Neeses, SC
Contact: Neeses Town Hall, 803-247-5811

North Fork Edisto Blueway

This 34-mile stretch of the Edisto River is in Orangeburg County and has been designated as a blueway for the public to use and enjoy. See Day Trip to the North Fork Blueway on page 23.
Contact: http://www.sctrails.net/Trails/ALLTRAILS/WaterTrails/EdistoNoFork.html

Orangeburg Cemetery

This cemetery was the first non-church-affiliated cemetery for African-Americans in Orangeburg County. It is listed on the National Register of Historic Places.
Hours/Dates of Operation: Dawn to Dusk

A Brown Water Snake sunning along the Edisto.

Location: Bull St., Orangeburg, SC
Contact: Orangeburg Parks and Recreation Department, 803-533-5870

Orangeburg National Fish Hatchery
The Orangeburg National Fish Hatchery is a warm-weather fish hatchery in Orangeburg. It has a one-mile observation walk and aquarium that are open to the public.
Hours/Dates of Operation: Monday-Friday, 8-3:30
Location: 427 Lake View Drive, Orangeburg, SC (just outside city limits)
Contact: Orangeburg National Fish Hatchery, 803-534-4828

Valentine's Cotton Gin and General Store
Visit this general store for "a peek into the past."
Location: Cope, SC
Contact: Store, 803-534-7105; Jo Helen Riley for tour, 803-534-0442

Unique Places to Stay

Kallaloo Tavern Inn & Suites
This inn is another bed and breakfast in the North Fork Region worth exploring.
Location: 4831 Columbia Road, Orangeburg, SC
Contact: 803-533-1166
Southern Lodge
The Southern Lodge is a hospitable hotel that provides an enjoyable stay at a great bargain.
Location: 3616 Saint Matthews Road, Orangeburg, SC
Contact: 803-531-7333

Festivals and Events

Grand American Coon Hunt
This annual coon hunt is held in Orangeburg County in early January. It is the largest field trial for coon dogs in the United States and is a qualifying event for the World Coon Hunt.
Location: Orangeburg County Fairgrounds, 350 Magnolia Street, Orangeburg, SC
Contact: Orangeburg Chamber of Commerce, 803-534-6821

Lexington County Peach Festival
This festival is held annually on the Fourth of July in Gilbert. It has been described as "the most elaborate, jam-packed, fun-filled, 'peachiest' festival around."
Location: Gilbert, SC

Orangeburg Festival of Roses
This annual, weekend-long festival celebrates the beginning of the rose blooming season the weekend before Mother's Day. The activities are centered in Orangeburg's Edisto Memorial Gardens, where thousands of roses bloom near the banks of the Edisto River. The festival also features an arts & crafts show as well as many other activities for adults and children.
Location: Edisto Memorial Gardens, Orangeburg, SC
Contact: www.festivalofroses.com, 800-545-6153

Rayrode Daze Festival
The town of Branchville celebrates its railroad history with this annual festival in September. You can enjoy arts, crafts, a parade, bands contests and more.
Location: 150 Edward St., Branchville, SC
Contact: 803-274-8454

Spring wisteria blossoms over the Edisto.

South Carolina Peanut Party

This annual party celebrates the boiled peanut. Held in August, it spans three days and is filled with events to honor the classic southern "goober."
Location: Pelion, SC
Contact: www.scpeanutparty.com

South Carolina Poultry Festival

The South Carolina Poultry Festival takes place on the second Saturday in May in Batesburg-Leesville, where it has been held since 1986.
Location: Main Street, Batesburg-Leesville, SC
Contact: Batesburg-Leesville Town Hall, 888-427-7273

Useful Web Sites for Exploring the North Fork

Bamberg County Chamber of Commerce:
www.bambergcountychamber.org

Capital City Lake Murray Country:
www.lakemurraycountry.com

Santee Cooper Country:
www.santeecoopercountry.org

The Ridge

Batesburg-Lees

39
191 193
23
Johnston 23 Ward Ridge Spring Monetta
1
Trenton
19 I-20
25 1
Hwy 21
302
191
118 Shaw Creek
1 78 Aiken 4
Burnettown 302 Aiken State Park
19 53 Sout.
78
New Ellenton
Redcliff State
Historic Site
39
278
SRS

South Fork	○ City/Town
Navigable Stream	Interstate
Swamp/Wetland	US Highway
Watershed	State Highway
○ Boat Ramp	State Park

N

Miles
0 2.5 5 10

The South Fork
of the Edisto River

Visit the South Fork of the Edisto, and . . .

. . . you will be struck by the extremes of the area. Go far west to experience the sophistication of Aiken, a former winter colony that is still a hub of horses and history. Travel north to Johnston and capture a glimpse of South Carolina's agricultural landscape that gives this farming town the title, "Peach Capital of the World." Go south to the small towns along US Highway 76 to see the best history and architecture that rural South Carolina has to offer.

Aiken County has a varied past. It was home to the first large, southern textile mill at Graniteville; many former textile towns still dot the landscape. Like much of South Carolina, textiles have been major forces in Aiken for most of its history.

The sandy soil in Aiken County has made it a perfect fit for the horse culture as well. In the 1800s, the town became a haven for the northern leisure class. The horse industry continues to be a big part of Aiken with several stables that produce quality thoroughbreds. A drive around Aiken County with its picket fences and lovely barns reflects the picturesque setting of an equestrian town. Each March, the Aiken Triple Crown is a major event for the horse racing community.

Aiken County is also the home of the Savannah River Site, the world's first facility for the making of thermo-nuclear materials. While the mission of the Site

A Slice of Scandinavia and Germany

Along the South Fork you will find locations bearing the names Denmark, Ehrhard, and Olar. These are just some of the small towns that show the Scandinavian influence in the South. These tight-knit communities in Bamberg and Orangeburg Counties were settled in the 1740s by immigrants seeking religious or political freedom and others for economic opportunities. These immigrants quickly became a vital part of the fabric of the communities. The South Fork also shows the influence of German settlers. As early as the mid-1800s, there were more than 10 Lutheran churches in the South Fork region of the state. German immigrants are primarily of the Lutheran denomination.

continues to evolve, its presence in Aiken has added to the vitality of the community.

DESTINATION: Johnston: *The Hub of the Ridge*

A unique geographic feature of southwestern South Carolina inspired the small town of Johnston's colorful nickname. "The Hub of the Ridge," as Johnston calls itself, refers to this small, friendly community's location at the meeting place of three river systems. These rivers flow away from The Ridge, a fertile plateau about 30 miles long between clay hills to the north and sand hills to the south.

Johnston also carries the title "Peach Capital of the World." The peach industry has been a major contributor to Johnston's economy since the early 1900s. It is said that today The Ridge produces about 60 percent of South Carolina's peaches —thanks in large part to Johnston.

The peaches in Johnston are not only

33

a big part of the economy, but they also add to the scenery. It is hard to imagine a better way to spend an afternoon than touring around the Johnston area once the peaches bloom in the spring. Add in the old southern homes and a revitalized Main Street and you have a great day trip. Plan your visit during the annual Peach Blossom Festival.

DAY TRIP: *God's Acre - Healing Springs*

A history and culture have grown up around "The Healing Springs," an artesian spring located in rural Barnwell County. Indian lore held that the water from the springs had healing powers. Tales from as early as the Revolutionary War period speak of its healing qualities.

Luke Boyleston, a deeply religious farmer, bought the springs at an auction. Upon his death in 1944, Mr. Boyleston's last will and testament deeded Healing Springs back to God and willed that no earthly owner ever again possess or control its waters. He believed God intended for the cool waters of the springs to always be a source of comfort for the afflicted. It is said that iced tea made with the spring water will keep indefinitely. People today still collect the water from this well.

Hours/Dates of Operation: Dawn to Dusk (free)

Location: Near SC #3, north of Blackville

DESTINATION: *Aiken*

Someone once said, "Aiken is not your typical small, southern town." He was right. Aiken has history, sophistication, and a whole lot more.

Aiken's unique character evolved from the city's founding as a healthful resort for wealthy Northerners who built "cottages," or magnificent summer homes

Be sure to find the artesian well at the Aiken State Natural Area.

n t e r e s t i n g   F a c t

Artesian Wells

There is an interesting artesian well near the canoe put-in at Aiken State Natural Area. This well, which was built by the Civilian Conservation Corps, flows endlessly all day, every day. In an artesian well, water rises from underground under its own pressure with no need for pumping. Artesian wells are often exploited because their water is fresh and easily available. Over time, these water sources can become unreliable. There is also some concern that pollutants, such as pesticides or nitrates, can seep into the aquifers. The artesian well at Aiken continues to flow and is safe to drink. Try a sip before you put your canoe in the Edisto.

and lavish parties.

When walking through the neighborhoods of Aiken, you will notice one elegant home after another located in leafy enclaves. Make sure to take a stroll along a city street to see how that half lives.

Downtown Aiken is designed around a series of boulevards, featuring gorgeous, tree-lined medians that quiet traffic and make the community a pedestrian-friendly place to spend an afternoon. Sometimes the boulevards make it difficult to figure out who has the right-of-way, but it doesn't seem to slow people down.

The international horse set hangs out in the country around Aiken at the Georgia-South Carolina border, where horse training and racing are major preoccupations. When you're driving, you might find yourself sharing the road with a horse and its mount. There's even a stoplight just for horses on Whiskey Road. Nearly a thousand horses winter and train in this area, and Aiken has two racetracks as well as polo grounds.

there. The fame of Aiken dates to the 1890s, when rich Northerners flocked there in winter and began erecting their lavish mansions. The "horsey" set amused themselves with horse shows, fox hunts,

History and nature meet at Aiken's Hopeland Gardens.

One of the Winter Colony "cottages" now houses the Aiken County Historical Museum. Because many of the other Winter Colony homes are still privately owned, one of the best ways to learn of Aiken's history and equestrian lifestyle is to take a tour on a Saturday morning. These tours are arranged through the Aiken Chamber of Commerce.

DAY TRIP:
Sounds Like Fun: Hopeland Gardens

After a few hours of hearty paddling on the Edisto River, you may be ready for a bit more leisurely pursuit. If that's the case, try Hopeland Gardens in Aiken. An hour spent strolling through the gardens is an excellent bookend to the more active pursuit on the Edisto.

It is hard to imagine a more elegant setting than these gardens. Surrounded by a serpentine brick wall, the dazzling 14 acres are filled with Southern botanical favorites and feature a brick path over a goldfish pool that leads to a balcony overlooking the lower part of the park.

Upon entering Hopeland Gardens, you immediately get the feeling that you are in a different world. During your trip there, imagine you are a wealthy industrialist in the 1920s who has come to South Carolina to spend the season. The landscaped surroundings and beautiful statuary will easily take you back in time.

Hopeland Gardens offers even more than a great spot for a leisurely stroll on a South Carolina spring day. It hosts a spring and summer concert series. The Thoroughbred Racing Hall of Fame is also located here, a reminder of Aiken's equestrian history and its special status as a winter colony. The adjacent Rye Patch Estate is now a popular place for weddings, receptions, parties, and business retreats. It is not otherwise open to the public.

Hours/Dates of Operation: 10-Dark, Year-Round
Location: 1700 Whisky Road, Aiken, SC (corner of Whiskey Road and Dupree Place)
Contact: City of Aiken, 803-642-7630

DAY TRIP: *Aiken State Natural Area*

Ask the ranger at Aiken State Natural Area what to do, and he will immediately say, "We are a river park...The Edisto River is what is special about the site . . . You don't often see a blackwater river like this up close."

The 1,100-acre Aiken State Natural Area is located 16 miles east of Aiken where the Edisto is free-flowing. Don't rush trying to get there, because the drive is part of the park's appeal. Crossing through timber land and rural communities, you catch a glimpse of pre-interstate South Carolina.

The land is a combination of river swamp and Carolina sandhills. There are campsites, nature trails, a meeting facility, and picnic shelter. The site offers a great way to spend an afternoon with the family and is just a short excursion from Aiken and Columbia.

Pay special attention to the park's administrative buildings built by the Civilian Conservation Corps in the 1930s. Many of South Carolina's pre-World War II park structures were built this way, and the ones at Aiken are among the best examples still in use.

Hours/Dates of Operation: Monday-Sunday, 9-6 (Friday-Sunday during daylight savings time, 9-9) (admission fee)
Location: 1145 State Park Road, Wagener, SC
Contact: Aiken State Natural Area, 803-649-2857

DAY TRIP: *Paddling the South Fork*

Don't forget that the Aiken State Natural Area is a river park. This is an opportunity to take advantage of the South Fork of the Edisto at its best. It's easy. The ranger will rent you a boat or a canoe. The canoe trail is a scenic, two-mile journey. The water moves swiftly so be ready for a good ride.

The surrounding land in Aiken State Natural Area is a combination of river swamp and dry sandhills, with the latter area offering evidence of an era when the ocean pushed this far inland. The park is extremely popular among fishermen and campers because of the easy river access and four spring-fed lakes.

Be sure to notice the Civilian Conservation Corp era architecture at Aiken State Natural Area.

It's historic and scenic downtown is what makes Aiken more than just another small southern town.

For the more hearty paddlers there are opportunities outside the park to enjoy the South Fork. The park offers easy access and a chance for novices to enjoy the river in a relaxed atmosphere.

More South Fork Attractions

Downtown Aiken

Surrounded by a one-of-a-kind parkway system and bordered by beautiful beds of flowers, the area offers unique dining and shopping choices, including art galleries, antiques, gift shops, a brew pub, and a variety of restaurants. Downtown is also home to the Aiken Center for the

Arts, the Aiken County Historical Museum, the Aiken Community Playhouse, and the Washington Center for the Performing Arts. **Contact:** Aiken Downtown Development Association, 803-649-2221

Aiken Center for the Arts

The Arts Center features gallery exhibits by local, state, and regional artists. Artists also display works for sale year-round in the gallery store.
Hours/Dates of Operation: Monday-Saturday, 10-4
Location: 122 Laurens Street SW, Aiken, SC
Contact: 803-641-9094

Aiken Community Playhouse

The Aiken Community Playhouse offers community theater at its best. The Playhouse has been in operation for more than 50 years. It is located in the Washington Center for the Performing Arts.
Location: 126 Newberry St. NW, Aiken, SC
Contact: 803-648-1438

Aiken County Historical Museum

This museum is housed in a 1931 winter colony mansion, one of only two open to the public.
Hours/Dates of Operation: Monday-Saturday, 10-5 ; Sunday, 2-5
Location: 433 Newberry St. SW, Aiken, SC
Contact: 803-642-2015

Aiken Gopher Tortoise Heritage Preserve

This preserve is home to the rare and state-listed endangered gopher tortoise, which has stumpy, elephantine hind feet. This approximately 1,500-acre preserve is the northernmost location inhabited by these large terrestrial tortoises.
Hours/Dates of Operation: Dawn to Dusk
Location: Off US 78, Windsor Road, Windsor, SC

Contact: www.sctrails.net, 803-734-3886

Aiken Winter Colony & Historic Districts

Aiken boasts three historic districts that are home to large estates with "cottages," many of which are on the National Register.
Hours/Dates of Operation: Saturday tours (reservations required and admission fee)
Location: Aiken, SC
Contact: 803-642-7631

Carolina Bay Park

Carolina Bay Park is a unique city park with a natural wetland that has had minimal improvements and offers maximum of tranquility. Leaflets (available at the park) provide a map, a guide to the trail, and seasonal information on what to look for in the woods and pond.
Location: Whiskey Road (SC 19) between Pine Log Road (SC 302) and Price Avenue, Aiken, SC
Contact: 803-648-0151

Cathedral Bay Heritage Wildlife Preserve

The Cathedral Bay Heritage Wildlife Preserve is an excellent example of the Carolina bay phenomenon. Found throughout the Atlantic Coastal Plain, these elliptical or

Cypress trees and cypress knees along the South Fork.

39

Photo courtesy of Bill Marshall and FRED.

oval basins are wetlands that vary in size and often support abundant wildlife. Access by wading and canoes allowed.

Location: SC 64, about 1.6 miles south of Olar, SC

Contact: SC Parks, Recreation and Tourism, http://www.discoversouthcarolina.com

Hitchcock Woods

Hitchcock Woods in Aiken is a nearly 2,000-acre wood maintained by the Hitchcock Foundation that offers natural beauty with hiking and riding trails.

Hours/Dates of Operation: Dawn to Dusk, Year-Round

Location: South Boundary Avenue Extension, Aiken, SC

Contact: Hitchcock Foundation, 803-642-0528

Montmorenci Vineyards

This family-owned business claims many award-winning wines. Grapes are grown in the vineyards and then turned into wine without the aid of machinery.

Hours/Dates of Operation: Wine tastings in gift shop (Friday-Saturday, 10-6)

Location: 2989 Charleston Hwy, Aiken, SC

Contact: 803-649-4870

Salley Historic District

The Salley Historic District consists of 60 properties in the downtown Salley area. The homes are Victorian and Art Deco. The town of Salley was founded in 1887, as a result of the railroad, and flourished until the 1930s.

Contact: Town of Salley Historical Society (H.N. Salley, Jr.), 803-258-3306

Wagener Museum

The Wagener Museum showcases Aiken's political, social, economic, and military history.

Hours/Dates of Operation: Friday, 8-5 pm; Saturday, 10-2; and Sunday, 2-5

Location: 12 Short Street, Wagener, SC

Contact: Wagener Town Hall, 803-564-3412

Wagon House

The Wagon House was built to house the Conestoga Wagon given to the town of Wagener by the state of South Carolina to use in its "Wagons to Wagener Festival" held each spring.

Hours/Dates of Operation: By appt. only

Location: Corner of Railroad Avenue and Earl Street, Wagener, SC

Contact: Wagener Town Hall, 803-564-3412

Washington Center for the Performing Arts

The Washington Center for the Performing Arts is a state-of-the-art facility for the theater-loving crowd. It seats approximately 300, plus it has a 32-seat Hospitality Suite/Balcony that is available for pre- and post-show receptions.

Location: 126 Newberry St. NW, Aiken, SC

Contact: 803-648-1438

Unique Places to Stay

The Hotel Aiken

The Hotel Aiken is in the heart of historic Aiken and dates back to 1898.

Location: 235 Richland Ave. West, Aiken, SC

Contact: 803-648-4265

The Willcox

The Willcox is a grand southern hotel where the well-to-do of the Gilded Age wintered to escape into Aiken's charm.
Location: 100 Colleton Avenue, Aiken, SC
Contact: 877-648-2200

Ziggy's Motel

Bamberg's Ziggy's Motel offers reasonable rates and is not far from the River.
Location: 2448 N. Main St, Bamberg, SC
Contact: 803-245-2429

Festivals and Events

Aiken Triple Crown

Three equestrian events held on consecutive weekends in March.
First Event: The Aiken Trials
Contact: Tournament Office
803-641-1111
Second Event: The Aiken Steeplechase
Contact: Mia Miller 803-648-9641
Third Event: Aiken Polo
Contact: Aiken Chamber of Commerce
803-641-1111

Annual South Carolina Governor's Frog Jump

This event is held each spring in Springfield as a qualifier for the Calveras County Jumping Frog competition that takes place in California and gets its name from the well-known Mark Twain short story. The contest has been held in small Springfield for over 40 years.
Location: Springfield, SC
Contact: Springfield Town Hall,
803-258-3152

Chitlin Strut

In November you can enjoy chitlin dinners, a parade, hawg-calling contests, a car show and more at this long-time festival.
Location: Salley, SC
Contact: The Towne of Salley (Phone) 803-258-3485 (Fax) 803-258-3484
Website: www.chitlinstrut.com

Dogwood Festival

This April event features food, rides, entertainment, games and contests, along with a spectacular fireworks display.
Location: Denmark, SC
Contact: Tyra Miller 803-275-3264

Johnston Peach Blossom Festival

This April event takes place on Johnston's Main Street and features a parade, crafts, and more.
Location: Johnston, SC
Contact: Giles Salbo 803-793-4533

Useful Web Sites for Exploring the South Fork

Aiken County Parks, Recreation and Tourism: www.aikencountysc.gov/tourism

City of Aiken: www.aiken.net

Hitchcock Woods: www.hitchcockwoods.org

National Wild Turkey Center and Museum Edgefield, SC, www.nwtf.org

Thoroughbred Country (Western South Carolina): www.tbredcountry.org

Photo courtesy of Bill Marshall and FRED.

Sandy beaches along the Edisto make good launching points for river trips.

41

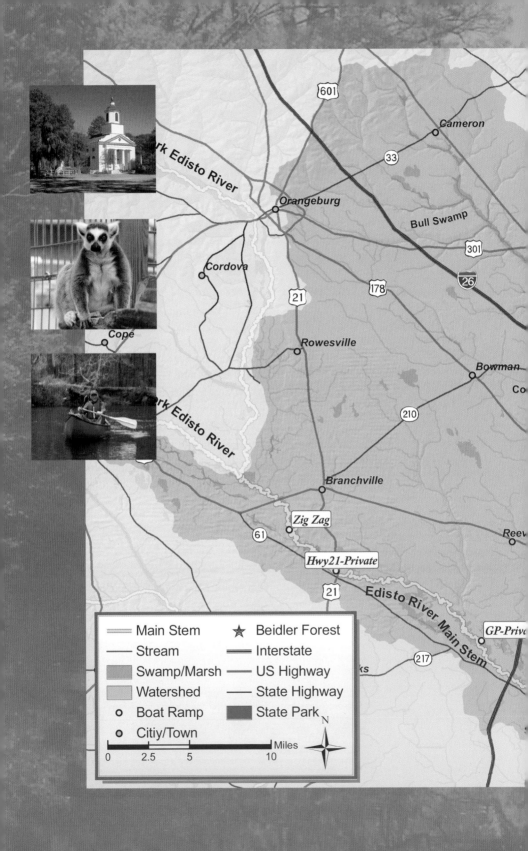

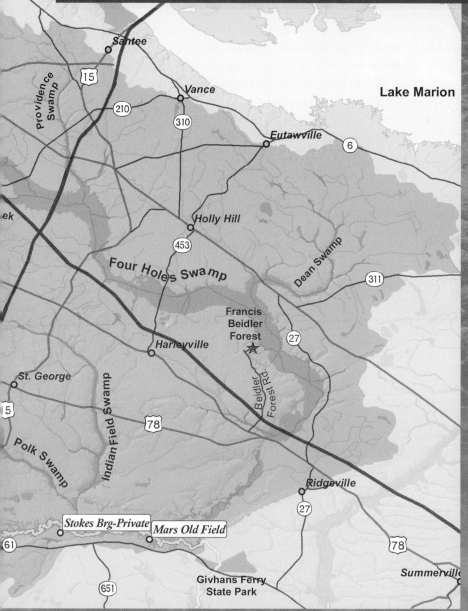

Most people think of the Main Stem . . .

. . . when planning trips to the Edisto River. After leaving the growing city of Orangeburg, there are miles and miles of undisturbed river that have become one of South Carolina's most popular outdoor recreation destinations.

The Main Stem is an area of transition. You are leaving one ecosystem and joining another. The rolling sand hills of The Ridge begin to give way to wetlands, swamps, and marshes. Just south of Walterboro, you enter the still undeveloped ACE Basin and coastal South Carolina.

The Colleton Historical Society Little Library constructed around 1820.

There are also cultural destinations along the way. The city of Walterboro is one example. It is an often overlooked historic part of the Palmetto State. Don't miss it. The buildings along these streets will make you think of rice planters from years ago.

The Beidler Forest and Four Holes Swamp could stand alone as a distinct part of the Edisto River. For organizational reasons, we included them within the Main Stem section. But, by all means, don't overlook Beidler Forest. It might be the greatest opportunity to see a natural swamp environment unchanged by man.

DESTINATION:
Walterboro

Driving into Walterboro from Interstate 95, it is easy to think of this small community of just 5,000 as just another highway rest stop. Keep on going into the historic downtown, and you soon discover that Walterboro is a rare glimpse of a southern culture that is slipping away.

From its beginnings, Walterboro has always been a destination for people seeking refuge and beauty. In the summer of 1784, owners of area rice plantations found a place for their summer homes and named it Hickory Valley. As this location grew, the people named it Walterboro after the two brothers who originally settled there, Paul and Jacob Walters.

The town, which was laid out in 1824, centers around the Colleton County Courthouse. It was designed by noted South Carolina architect Robert Mills. Use the court house as a starting point for your tour. Look out for the historic nineteenth century buildings that grace the community. Historic districts help keep much of the charm of early Walterboro viable. It is definitely worth spending some time walking around.

Walterboro can be a welcomed change of pace for those who have spent several days in the wild beauty of the ACE Basin and surrounding area. By coming into Walterboro, you are able to experience what life would have been like a couple of hundred years ago.

Located downtown are the Colleton County Museum and the South Carolina Artisan's Center. The museum is located in the old jail and is an interesting building in its own right. The South Carolina Artisan's Center has quickly acquired a reputation for featuring the best of the state's homegrown arts and crafts. It is great for picking up gifts for those back home.

Make sure you include a visit to the Colleton Historical Society Little Library, originally constructed circa 1820. This beautiful building and the surrounding neighborhood are, in and of themselves, well worth the time it takes to get to them from the interstate.

Colleton State Park is canoe and kayak headquarters.

DAY TRIP:
Colleton State Park

To many, the thought of canoeing or kayaking a great river like the Edisto is a mixed proposition. It sounds fun, but it also sounds intimidating. Colleton State Park is the perfect place to face your fears of paddling on the Edisto.

Colleton State Park was built by the Civilian Conservation Corps in the 1930s next to the Edisto River in order to encourage the River's use by the public. Just five minutes from Interstate 95, you have access to a 35-acre park that has become a place to teach people how to enjoy a variety of water activities. Today, the park still features much of the original

architecture. There is a short interpretive trail and a nice campground to orient visitors to this history.

The park offers opportunities for everyone, from the novice to the most experienced river rat. Beginners can rent a canoe or kayak there, learn how to paddle, and schedule a guided trip. It's a one-stop shopping spot for those interested in experiencing the River. Campers, fishermen, canoeists, and other outdoor enthusiasts use the park to enjoy the peaceful and relaxing blackwater. Colleton State Park is designated an official canoe and kayak trail.

A great time to visit the park is during the Edisto Riverfest, an annual festival held the second weekend of June. The festival offers numerous guided canoe trips, educational programs, workshops, exhibits, and music.

Location: 147 Wayside Lane, Canadys, SC
Contact: Colleton State Park, 843-538-8206

I n t e r e s t i n g   F a c t

The Tuskegee Airmen

During World War II, the US military used the Walterboro Army Airfield as a training facility for the famous World War II Tuskegee Airmen, the first Black fighter pilots. They trained in Walterboro for three years before being sent into battle.

DAY TRIP: *Edisto River Canoe and Kayak Trail*

Outdoor enthusiasts are always looking for new, scenic places to experience. If you want to see one of South Carolina's true natural wonders, try the Edisto River Canoe and Kayak Trail. It is a great and easy way to see the River.

The Edisto River Canoe and Kayak Trail is a 56-mile trail on the Main Stem of the Edisto River. It has its foundation in two South Carolina state parks: Colleton and Givhans Ferry. Both offer camping and picnicking spots and are great resources for accessing the River in a safe and structured way.

Contact the Edisto River Canoe and Kayak Trail Commission to arrange a canoe trip along the Trail. This dedicated volunteer group has developed a good reputation for promoting and protecting the Edisto. They can also put you in contact with guides and other services to make your trip enjoyable.

If you paddle quietly, you can see

Photo courtesy of Jim Wescot and ERCK.

Interesting Fact

Numbered Duck Boxes

Rivers have always been used as nature's highways, but paddlers on the Edisto have taken this a step further. When floating along the 56-mile Edisto River Canoe and Kayak Trail, pay special attention to numbers painted on the duck boxes. They are telling you how many miles you are from the Atlantic Ocean, similar to a modern-day mile marker along an interstate highway. Several years ago the Trail Commission recognized that there was a need for mileage signs to help direct paddlers. The duck boxes were a way to provide direction without using traditional signage that would clutter the River. Duck boxes provide habitat for waterfowl and are the perfect location for mileage signs. They are also a useful conversation starter for river guides

various kinds of wildlife, including egrets, great blue herons, and ducks. To add educational value to your trip, take along a guide book and learn about the different species. The Commission's canoe guides are also good sources of information.

While the Trail has grown in popularity over the years, it still offers a peaceful way to spend an afternoon. Leave your cell phones and daily worries on the River's bank and float away from civilization. You may see a johnboat filled with fishermen or a group of kayakers leisurely enjoying the River. You will not see condominiums or bright lights.

Be on the lookout for one of the Edisto's famous sandbars for a quick lunch or afternoon nap. You will be surprised how far away you have traveled from everyday stress.

Contact: Edisto River Canoe and Kayak Commission, PO Box 1763, Walterboro, SC 29488, www.edistoriver.org.

Canoeing Instruction

The guides at the Edisto Canoe and Kayak Commission are experts at maneuvering the tight turns and downed trees on the River. They lead tours, give lessons, and introduce the River to thousands each year. Commission guides Joe Grange and Danny Burbage have some advice for people looking to be good canoeists:

1) Learn and practice good skills. There is no substitute for learning the correct strokes and putting them into practice.

2) Be attentive. Rivers and wind have their own agendas. Good canoeists respect these forces of Mother Nature.

3) Act in concert with the River. Why fight a river? It will win in the end.

4) Relax. It makes for better paddling. After all, you are on a river.

Mastering good water skills is a challenging, yet a fun and rewarding process. It may also be spiritual. According to Danny, "There is great joy in learning the skills to make a boat work well in a river."

DAY TRIP: *See Bee City*

One of the most unusual and interesting stops along the Main Stem of the Edisto is Bee City, the tucked-away honeybee farm, petting zoo, gift shop, and restaurant that is located three miles west of Givhans Ferry State Park. It's hard to describe Bee City in a few words.

It all started with bees. The tupelo trees growing along the Edisto River produce one of the finest honeys in North America. Bee City uses the work of these insects to make super honey. It is quite an education to watch such small creatures making one of nature's most perfect products.

The farm's uniqueness has made it a prime destination for school trips. Making the most of the public's interest, the owners opened one of the most unusual petting zoos. From monkeys to llamas, there are animals of every curiosity at Bee City.

Be sure to allow time to have a meal at the Bee City Café. Known for its fresh seafood, the food is as interesting as the décor. The room is filled with local relics. Murals from the 1950s give it a festive atmosphere.

See Bee City; it will not disappoint.

Interesting Fact

What is an Apiary?

An apiary is a place for honeybee hives. Some farmers provide free apiary sites, because their crops need the pollination the bees provide. Some apiaries, like Bee City, are involved in the commercial production of honey or other products. There are beekeepers and apiaries—from hobbyists to commercial —in every state.

Atlantic Ocean.

Four Holes Swamp is different from the usual river bottoms you will find along the Edisto. It is, in fact, a swamp-stream system fed largely by springs and runoff from surrounding higher areas. There is no one channel to follow, yet swamp water moves slowly and relentlessly seaward through a network of waterways. Geologists believe this low depression is probably a remnant of an ancient estuary, its shape carved by tides and wind at a time when the Atlantic Ocean covered much of the present coastal plain.

Beidler Forest contains the largest remaining virgin stand of bald cypress and

There is also a gift shop where you can buy honey and other memorabilia. With all of its eccentricities, Bee City is a great way to spend an afternoon on the River.
Hours/Dates of Operation: Tuesday-Thursday, 9-5; Friday-Saturday, 9-6 (field trips by appointment)
Location: US Hwy 61 (three miles west of Givhans Ferry State Park), Cottageville, SC
Contact: Bee City, 843-835-5912, www.beecity.net.

DAY TRIP:
Francis Beidler Forest in Four Holes Swamp

A day trip to Beidler Forest is a great way to understand a Lowcountry swamp. The 11,500-acre sanctuary is co-owned by the Nature Conservancy and Audubon Society, two of the country's preeminent conservation groups.

It is hard to imagine a more interesting part of the Edisto River Basin than Beidler Forest. It sits in Four Holes Swamp, the largest tributary of the Edisto River. Four Holes Swamp begins as a swamp-stream system separated by a low divide from the Congaree River Valley. After winding 62 miles through four counties, the black swamp water joins the Edisto River to complete its journey to the

tupelo gum trees in the world. Ancient groves of cypress trees stretch skyward, and many reach a height equivalent to a ten-story building. Oak, ash, tupelo, and black gum trees create an under-story that grows as high as 70 feet.

The Audubon Society manages the Francis Beidler Forest in an environmentally sensitive manner. Public visitation, education, and research uses of the forest conform to preservation of the ecosystem. During your visit, notice that all facilities were planned to soften the impact on vegetation, minimize grading and water runoff, and prevent

Who was Francis Beidler?

You might know the Beidler name as just a place on an interstate exit directing tourists to the Audubon Society's magnificent sanctuary. To students of South Carolina's past, the name Francis Beidler played an incredibly important part of the Palmetto State's conservation history.

Trace the history of land ownership in Orangeburg, Calhoun, Berkeley, and Dorchester Counties, and the name Beidler shows up repeatedly. Beidler purchased lands in these counties for their timber value. Francis Beidler's Santee River Cypress Lumber Company acquired much of the land around the Congaree and Santee Rivers to log the cypress trees found in the bottomland forest. It was quite an operation and made Beidler one of the great lumber barons of his day.

Beidler also promoted conservation of South Carolina's forests. A supporter of President Theodore Roosevelt, he championed conservation of this natural resource. After Beidler's death, his family began to liquidate his estate. The prospect of the sale of the property drew the attention of local conservationists. The National Audubon Society and The

Nature Conservancy ultimately raised funds to acquire 3,415 acres as a sanctuary.

It has been quite a journey for the Beidler Forest from commercial forest to a protected sanctuary. The story continues as the sanctuary has grown from a core of 3,500 acres to almost 12,000 today. Each step on this journey is a continuation in the transformation of Francis Beidler's vision.

any pollutants from entering the swamp ecosystem. Even the parking spaces slip inconspicuously between the trees.

Start your trip at the visitors center, the gateway to the sanctuary. The building is barrier-free for persons with disabilities and is raised on poles to allow water to pass under the building. No roots were cut when making the foundation, allowing trees to be part of the visitor's experience.

You will spend most of your time on the 6,500-foot boardwalk that traverses a small portion of the majestic cypress-tupelo swamp. As you enter this natural cathedral, remember that it is an area for quiet, solitude, and tranquility. Native wildlife abounds throughout the year, yet often eludes observation by casual visitors. The wilderness sets its own terms for your visit.[8]

Hours/Dates of Operation: Tuesday-Sunday, 9-5 (Closed Mondays, Thanksgiving, December 24, 25, 31, and New Year's Day. Admission charged.)
Location: 336 Sanctuary Road, Harleyville, SC
Contact: 843-462-2150
Other Useful Information: No camping. No pets on the walk. No food facilities in the sanctuary. Canoe trips, night walks, and other activities are available in-season and by reservation only.

More Main Stem/Four Holes Swamp Attractions

Bedon-Lucas House

The Bedon-Lucas House is a pre-Civil War home that Colleton County Historical and Preservation Society purchased in the 1990s. This home is one of the key historic sites in Walterboro.
Hours/Dates of Operation: March-November, Thursday-Saturday, 1-4
Location: 205 Church Street, Walterboro, SC
Contact: 843-549-9633

Colleton County Courthouse

The Colleton County Courthouse is a Greek Revival building designed by the

8. National Audubon Society. *The Francis Beidler Forest in Four Holes Swamp, A Self Guided Tour of the Boardwalk,* 1978, p. 3.

What are Cypress Knees?

According to the folks at Beidler Forest, the most frequently asked question is, "What are cypress knees?" It is easy to see why the question is popular. The knees stand out on a trip through the cypress swamp. They come in all shapes and sizes.

No one is certain about the true function of cypress knees. The traditional theory is that they serve as anchors to keep the trees steady in wet soils, sort of like a counterweight. Others think they function like snorkels, bringing air to a tree's root system. A new explanation gaining in popularity is that they are storage banks for starches. No theory has been proven, so take your pick.

Four Holes Swamp

Nobody knows for sure how Four Holes Swamp earned its name. Some think it came from the four fishing lakes used by the Yemasee Indians. Others believe the name comes from four "holes" through the swamp that form seasonal, dry passageways, which were used by early pioneers. The true story has been lost to history. You can choose your own.

Location: 239 N. Jefferies Blvd., Walterboro, SC
Contact: 843-549-2303

Eutaw Springs Battlefield

The Eutaw Springs Battlefield marks the last major battle of the American Revolution on South Carolina soil.
Location: Highway 6, Eutawville, SC

Great Swamp Sanctuary

The Great Swamp Sanctuary is more than 800 acres of braided-creek hardwood flats bottom land with three miles of hiking and bicycling trails and is also popular for canoeing.
Location: Detreville Street, Walterboro, SC
Contact: City of Walterboro, 843-549-2545

Pon Pon Chapel

Pon Pon Chapel is a rare opportunity to see the ruins of a pre-Revolutionary War

famous South Carolina architect Robert Mills. It hosted the state's first public nullification meeting in 1828.
Hours/Dates of Operation: Monday-Friday, 8-5
Location: 101 Hampton Street, Walterboro, SC
Contact: Courthouse, 843-549-5791;

Colleton Museum

The Colleton Museum is housed in the "Old Jail," which is the third jail in the county's history. The museum is listed in the National Register of Historic Places. It features exhibits on the history of Colleton County, as well as traveling art exhibits.
Hours/Dates of Operation: Tuesday-Friday, 10-5; Saturday, Noon-4

This tree along the River's edge shows the signs of wildlife.

Swamp Genius: *Mike Dawson*

To many people, a swamp is a mystifying place filled with dark spaces and scary animals. To Beidler Forest education director Mike Dawson, a swamp is a place of wonder.

"I have been to a lot of scenic places with panoramic views," says Dawson. "In the swamp you get up close to natural beauty. I learn new, interesting, scary, and bizarre stuff each trip into the swamp." Mike has some advice for novices. "Don't visit with any preconceived notions about swamp life. Be prepared to have your eyes opened."

Wildlife can be hard to spot your first time in Four Holes Swamp. Mike offers a few tips for observing the wonders of the animal world:

• Walk quietly.

• Remember that wildlife does not want you to find it. So you have to know how and where to look.

• Finding wildlife takes skill in observing what is out of place. A dash of color in a green canopy is a giveaway. Follow that color to the movement of wildlife.

Mike has been leading tours and teaching about Beidler Forest for years. He writes a column for the local paper under the name "Swamp Genius." He has been observing wildlife so long he can tell the difference between splashes in the water. For example, "turtles go 'splash' when they hit the water. Fish go 'splish' or 'plop.'" That's what Mike is . . . a swamp genius who knows South Carolina's Four Holes Swamp through and through.

Pon Pon Chapel

structure. The chapel was originally built in 1725. It is listed in the National Register. The Reverend John Wesley preached two sermons there.

Location: Parker's Ferry Road, Jacksonboro, SC

Contact: Colleton County Historical and Preservation Society, 843-549-9633

Slave Relic Museum

The Slave Relic Museum displays 300 years of authentic slave artifacts made and used by enslaved Africans from 1750 to the mid-1800s.

Hours/Dates of Operation: Monday-Thursday, 9:30-5; Saturday, 10-3

Location: 208 Carn Street, Waterboro, SC

Contact: 843-549-9130

South Carolina Artisans Center

The South Carolina Artisans Center is the official folk art and craft center in the state. It is housed in an eight-room Victorian cottage and showcases more than 240 juried South Carolina artists.

Hours/Dates of Operation: Saturday, 10-5:30; Sunday, 1-5

Location: 334 Wichman Street, Walterboro, SC

Contact: 843-549-0011

Tomb of Isaac Hayne

Isaac Hayne was a Revolutionary War hero who lived near Jacksonboro. His tomb is maintained as a state historic site.

Location: Off Hwy 64, near Jacksonboro, SC

Contact: Colleton State Park, 843-538-8206

Tuskegee Airmen Monument

This monument honors the dedication of the Tuskegee Airmen.

Location: Walterboro Army Airfield Memorial Park, Hwy 17-A at the Walterboro Airport, Walterboro, SC

Contact: Walterboro Airport, 843-549-9595

Walterboro Historic District

The Walterboro Historic District offers visitors a glimpse of the town's historic past with its architecture and southern charm.

Unique Places to Stay

Country Hearth Inn

Country Hearth Inn is a perfect stopover for a quick rest in St. George.
Location:104 Interstate Drive, St. George, SC
Contact: 843-563-2277

Hampton House Bed and Breakfast

If you stay at the Hampton House Bed and Breakfast, be sure to ask to see the Forde doll houses. There are more than 50 doll houses and antique dolls.
Location: 500 Hampton St., Walterboro, SC
Contact: 843-542-9498

Old Academy Bed & Breakfast

The Old Academy was originally built and used as Walterboro's first school house. It dates back to 1834.
Location: 904 Hampton St., Walterboro, SC
Contact: 843-549-3232

Festivals and Events

Colleton County Rice Festival

This festival celebrates Colleton County's rice planting heritage with a fireworks display, entertainment, arts and crafts, food vendors and more.
Location: Walterboro, SC
Contact: Bennie Ordel 843-549-1079
Website: www.ricefestival.org

Edisto Riverfest

This June festival offers a variety of paddling workshops, canoe/kayak trips, live music, and food.
Location: Colleton State Park on the Edisto River
Contact: Ileen Grange at 843-693-3161.
Website: www.edistoriver.org

St. George's World Grits Festival

This festival is held every April and features the "Rolling in Grits" competition. The winner is the contestant who covers himself with the most grits in ten seconds.
Location: St. George, SC
Contact: Rodger Myers 843-681-7635

Useful Web Sites for Exploring Colleton County

Audubon Center at Beidler Forest:
www.beidlerforest.com

Colleton County Chamber of Commerce: www.colletoncounty.org

South Carolina Artisans Center, Walterboro: www.
southcarolinaartisanscenter.org

Birds like this Prothonotary Warbler demonstrate the vibrant colors of nature along the Edisto.

ACE Basin & Edisto Island

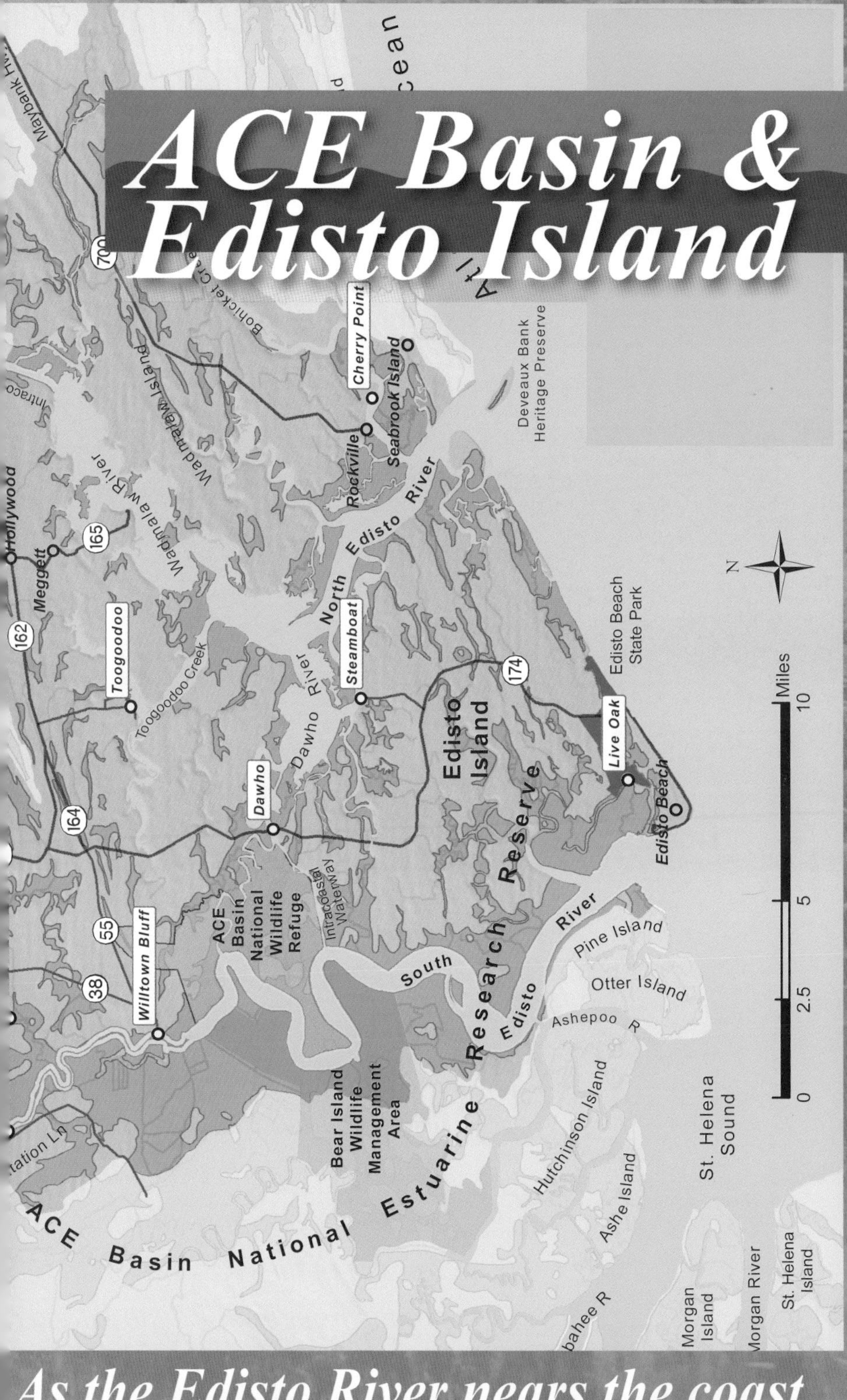

As the Edisto River nears the coast, . . .

Maybank Hwy

Bohicket Cr

700

Intraco

Wadmalaw Island

Wadmalaw River

Hollywood

Meggett

165

162

Toogoodoo

Toogoodoo Creek

164

55

38

Willtown Bluff

Station Ln

ACE Basin National Estuarine

Cherry Point

Seabrook Island

Rockville

North Edisto River

Atl

Ocean

Deveaux Bank Heritage Preserve

Steamboat

Dawho River

Dawho

ACE Basin National Wildlife Refuge

Intracoastal Waterway

Edisto Island

174

Live Oak

Edisto Beach State Park

Edisto Beach

N

Research Reserve

South

Edisto River

Bear Island Wildlife Management Area

Pine Island

Otter Island

Ashepoo R

Hutchinson Island

Ashe Island

St. Helena Sound

Morgan River

Morgan Island

St. Helena Island

bahee R

ACE Basin National

Miles

10

5

2.5

0

. . . it joins with two other rivers, the Ashepoo and Combahee, to create an estuarine system of wetlands and tidal creeks. Differentiating between land and water becomes difficult. You are in the ACE Basin and not far from both Edisto Island and the end of the River itself.

Taking its name from the three rivers that join together to form this pristine environment—the Ashepoo, Combahee, and Edisto—the ACE Basin is one of the largest undeveloped estuaries on the east coast. It is home to approximately 350,000 acres of diverse plants and animals, including several endangered and threatened species, such as bald eagles, wood storks, ospreys, and loggerhead sea turtles. This natural treasure has been designated a world-class ecosystem by the Nature Conservancy. It owes its preservation to partnerships among government agencies, private conservation groups, and landowners, which first banded together in the late 1980s to ensure protection of the Basin's natural state.

Still farther down the River emerges Edisto Island. The rural communities on Edisto serve as a reminder that South Carolina's coast was once totally undeveloped and revolved around agriculture and fishing, industries now threatened with development. Rural Edisto Island serves as a buffer to Edisto Beach. Surrounded by thousands of acres of undeveloped land, Edisto is the perfect place to watch birds and sunsets. Edisto has cultivated a reputation as a quiet family island.

I n t e r e s t i n g   F a c t

Levee Trunks [9]

While you're in the ACE Basin, look out for some interesting wooden structures under the dikes. They are called "trunks" and are used to move water from one side of the dike to the other. These simple examples of elegant engineering have their origins in the area's early rice culture when planters used hollow logs to move water through dikes. The British brought in Dutch engineers to design ways to manage water levels. The trunks use swing doors that can be raised to control the flow of water. By opening the doors during low or high tide, water will flow from one side of the levee to the other. Land managers use this simple technique to manipulate the difference in water levels.

9. Pete Laurie, *"Ageless Structures," SC Wildlife,* Jan.-Feb. 2006, p. 34.

DESTINATION:
Edisto Beach

Edisto is the perfect place to come for those looking for a relaxing and slow-paced get-away. How is it possible for there to be a beach like Edisto with the ever-increasing demand to develop coastal locations? Maybe it is, in part, because of its remoteness. It lies at the end of a road that seems to go on forever. When you finally reach the island and beach, you are actually at the end of Highway 174. Don't be fooled, though, into thinking there will not be much to do on Edisto other than walk on the beach.

DAY TRIP:
Paddling the ACE Basin

At first glance the wondrous ACE Basin can be a confusing place to visit. A good way to experience this natural area is from the water by canoe or kayak.

Expect to see a lot during your trip. Nesting bald eagles can be seen during the winter. Alligators can be seen sunning themselves on the banks. Don't be afraid of these creatures, but show them some respect. Birdwatchers will tell you the spring and summer months are great for seeing tropical migrant songbirds.

There are over a thousand acres of rice fields in the ACE Basin. As you float along, try to imagine the immense labor and sacrifice that went into creating these early parts of the Lowcountry economy. The concept is almost too overwhelming to comprehend.

DAY TRIP: *Edisto Beach State Park*

Built by the Civilian Conservation Corps, Edisto Beach State Park provides visitors the state's longest system of disability-friendly hiking and biking trails. The park also has an environmental education center that highlights the natural history of the island and the surrounding ACE Basin. For those on a limited budget, and, for that matter, anyone interested in experiencing the great outdoors on Edisto, the park has several campground facilities. An oceanfront campground sits in the midst of a palmetto-lined beach. The park also offers a more remote campground deep in the maritime forest. Comfortable cabins are available as well, which offer visitors a front-row view of miles of pristine marshland. Read more about the park's Interpretive Center on page 63.

Location: 8377 State Cabin Road, Edisto Island, SC

Contact: For reservations, visit www.reserveamerica.com. For more information, visit www.DiscoverSouthCarolina.com, or call 866-345-7275.

DAY TRIP: *Shell Collecting and Fossil Hunting*

Edisto is a favorite location to collect shells and fossils. Miles of beach provide good picking for those willing to comb the sand. Take a stroll on the beach

Irvin's Favorite Birds of the Ace Basin

Irvin Pitts is best known as the "Chief of Interpretation" at South Carolina State Parks. He is in charge of making sure that our parks are well designed and well cared for. What some people don't know is that Irvin is also one of the best birders in South Carolina. Irvin knows birds, and the ACE Basin has plenty of them. Here is a list of Irvin's favorites.

Tundra Swan (Cygnus columbianus)

With a wingspan of nearly seven feet, this large, long-necked waterfowl winters in shallow estuaries, lakes, and ponds along the vast marshes of the ACE Basin region in South Carolina. Flocks also frequent wet agricultural fields where they graze on a variety of grasses.

Yellow-crowned Night-heron (Nyctanassa violacea)

During the day, this stocky, nocturnal heron is more likely to be found resting near water in small trees or clumps of thick vegetation. They are typically active at night, searching shallow water for crayfish, snails, and various aquatic amphibians in a variety of wetland habitats.

Barred Owl (Strix varia)

The Barred Owl is a common inhabitant of swampy woodlands and heavily forested river bottoms. This stocky, medium-to-large owl is easily recognized by its streaked brown plumage, round head, and dark brown eyes. The distinctive call of the Barred Owl is a series of clear, accented hoots that end with a slurred, descending "awwwl" note.

Downy Woodpecker (Picoides pubescens)

This black-and-white plumaged bird is our smallest and most common woodpecker. The widespread Downy Woodpecker is a year-round inhabitant of a variety of woodland habitats. This species uses its stiff tail feathers and chisel-like bill to search beneath bark and dead branch stubs for well-hidden insects.

Yellow-rumped Warbler (Dendroica coronata)

The Yellow-rumped Warbler is South Carolina's most abundant and best known wintering wood warbler. This small songbird congregates in large flocks at coastal wax myrtle thickets. In both winter and spring, the Yellow-rumped Warbler plumage is characterized by a yellow crown, sides, and distinctive rump patch.

The ACE Basin Interpretive Center helps visitors understand the Edisto Beach area.

near the tidal inlet after a storm, and you are guaranteed to find a treasure trove of Edisto's present and past sea life.

More ACE Basin and Edisto Island Attractions

ACE Basin Interpretive Center at Edisto State Park

The best place to begin your visit to the ACE Basin is the Edisto State Park Interpretive Center. The center is located a stone's throw from a super wilderness trail. You are that close to nature. It's not unheard of to spot deer or other critters. You will find a variety of exhibits, programs, and services at the center that provide an overview of the ACE Basin and South Carolina Lowcountry. It explains the different ecosystems along the Edisto River, showing how the environment changes as it approaches the sea. A favorite attraction for children is the model ocean research vessel. Curious minds can go aboard and see how real scientists work. You can also learn about the endangered loggerhead sea turtle there. Watching these wonders lay their eggs and retreat into the sea is a special occasion along the coast. The center is managed by the SC Department of Parks, Recreation & Tourism and Department of Natural Resources.

Hours/Dates of Operation: Tuesday-Saturday, 9-4

Location: 8377 State Cabin Road (near Live Oak Boat Landing off Hwy. 174, about 50 miles south of Charleston)

A Tri-colored Heron looking for supper.

Contact: 843-869-4430 or
www.DiscoverSouthCarolina.com

Beach Rentals

Only a few lucky visitors own a
home on Edisto Island. Most people rent
by the week. Contact the local Chamber
of Commerce for a complete listing of
available houses, or call Edisto Sales and
Rentals Realty 866-856-6538.

Bear Island Wildlife Management Area

The Bear Island Wildlife Management
Area is managed by the SC Department
of Natural Resources to provide quality
habitat for wintering waterfowl, other
wetland wildlife, and upland game
and non-game species. It also provides
recreational opportunities for the hunting
and non-hunting public.

Hours/Dates of Operation: February 1-
October 14, Monday-Saturday
Location: Off US Highway 17, approximately
13 miles down Bennett's Point Road
Contact: SC Department of Natural
Resources, 843-844-8957

Caw Caw Interpretive Center

The Caw Caw Interpretive Center is
situated on a 654-acre site rich in natural,
cultural, and historical resources. The
land was once part of a 5,500-acre rice

plantation and was home to enslaved
Africans who applied their technology
and skills in agriculture to carve a highly
successful series of rice fields out of this
cypress swamp. The center offers a host of
recreational and educational opportunities.

Hours/Dates of Operation: Wednesday-
Friday, 9-3; Saturday-Sunday, 9-5
Location: 5200 Savannah Hwy, Ravenel, SC
Contact: Caw Caw Interpretive Center,
843-889-8898

Deveaux Bank Heritage Preserve

This estuarine island at the mouth of
the North Edisto can be reached only by
boat. It encompasses approximately 25
acres in Charleston County and is one of the
most significant sea and shore bird nesting
areas in South Carolina. The preserve was
established to protect the nesting habitat.

Hours/Dates of Operation: Contact the
SC Department of Natural Resources,
because parts of the preserve are always
closed to the public, and some are open
only for part of the year.
Contact: SC Department of Natural
Resources, 803-734-3886

Donnelley Wildlife Management Area

This wildlife management area was
named in honor of the late Gaylord and

Dorothy Donnelley for their contributions to the ACE Basin Project. The SC Department of Natural Resources manages the area to provide optimum habitat for a wide variety of wildlife and to provide public recreation and education. The area has two designated nature trails and miles of dirt roads for hikers and bicyclists.

Hours/Dates of Operation: Monday-Saturday, 8-5

Location: Eastern Colleton County near Green Pond, SC (Main entrance is immediately north of the junction of SC 303 and US 17.)

Contact: SC Department of Natural Resources, 843-844-8957

Edisto Island Museum

Nestled in the beach and the vast ACE Basin is the interesting Edisto Island Museum. Focusing on the 300-year history of the Island, it offers exhibits on everything from Native Americans to European settlement to the African slave trade. It is a small building chock full of South Carolina history. It also presents information on the conservation and preservation of Edisto Island.

Hours/Dates of Operation: Tuesday-Saturday, 1-4

Location: 8123 Chisholm Plantation Road, Edisto Island, SC

Contact: 843-869-1954

Edisto Island Serpentarium

This one-of-a-kind "museum" houses live sea turtles, snakes, alligators, and lizards in outdoor and indoor habitats.

Dates/Hours of Operation: Monday-Saturday, 10-6

Location: 1374 Highway 174, Edisto Island, SC

Contact: 843-869-1171

Edisto Nature Trail

Long before the ACE Basin effort opened this wetlands wonderland to the public, the Edisto Nature Trail was a popular stopping point for people wanting to catch a glimpse of the Lowcountry. The MeadWestvaco Corporation maintains the Trail, which is an easy one-mile loop, with an inner loop that extends the distance by a half mile. Sections of the trail wind through a typical Lowcountry forest of mature pines, hardwoods, and bald cypress. The brochure available at the trailhead orients a self-guided tour. Nature enthusiasts can identify almost 60 varieties of flora and fauna. An old railroad bed provides an excellent view of the forest, the historic King's Highway, and an old railroad tram.

Location: US Highway 17 north of Jacksonboro

Contact: MeadWestvaco, 843-871-5000

Ernest F. Hollings ACE Basin National Wildlife Refuge

This refuge encompasses more than 11,000 acres. The Edisto unit is housed in the Grove Plantation House, which was built in 1828 and is listed on the National Register of Historic Places. The US Fish and Wildlife Service manages the refuge.

Hours/Dates of Operation: Monday–Friday, 7:30-4

Location: 8675 Willtown Road off SC 174 (near Adams Run, SC)

Contact: ACE NWR, 843-889-3084

The Old Post Office is famous for nights out on Edisto Beach.

Island Bikes & Outfitters

A great way to explore Edisto Beach is on a bike. You can rent one at Island Bikes & Outfitters. There is also other recreational equipment available.
Location: 140 Jungle Road, Edisto Beach, SC
Contact: 843-869-4444

Morgan Island aka "Monkey Island"

Known as "Monkey Island," this island is home to rhesus monkeys used for research by the federal government. Visitors are not allowed on the island, but there are boat tours that will bring you nearby to take a look at and listen to these primates.

The Old Post Office Restaurant

It is dangerous to list a restaurant on a "must-visit" places list. However, the Old Post Office has become such an institution that one cannot mention Edisto without recommending a meal there. The restaurant is actually in an old post office building. The white clapboard building was renovated in 1988 into what has become a landmark and general center of the community. True to its community, seafood entrees are its signature dishes. But there is always something delicious for the meat lover, too. In the laid-back atmosphere that you find on Edisto, the fine-dining experience of the Old Post Office is quite a change. While it can be pricey, it is worth the visit.
Location: 1448 Highway 174, Edisto Island, SC
Contact: 843-869-2339

Unique Places to Stay

Fairfield Ocean Ridge Resort

Located on Edisto Beach, the Fairfield Ocean Ridge Resort dubs itself as a "lazy resort." Stay there and see for yourself.

Looking for a Night Out on the Town?

Edisto is unique in a state known for beaches and "beach life." It is a place of little commercialization with responsible development. It is perfect for those in search of rest and relaxation. At the same time, Edisto is less than 100 miles from the livelier locations of Charleston and Hilton Head. But most visitors find that there is so much to do and experience on Edisto that they don't want to leave the Island, even for a day.

Location: 1 King Cotton Rd., Edisto Beach, SC
Contact: 843-869-2561

Sanctuary at Kiawah Island Golf Resort

This hotel offers luxurious accommodations and is surrounded by 10 miles of unspoiled beach.
Location: One Sanctuary Beach Drive, Kiawah Island, SC
Contact: 800-654-2924 (reservations); 843-768-2121 (hotel)

Southerly Bed and Breakfast

You can find this B&B on Yonges Island, nestled next to the ACE Basin and just 20 minutes from Charleston. It sits on six acres, and while it offers visitors nearby beaches and golf courses, it is still a haven for nature lovers.
Location: 7760 Little Britton Road, Yonges Island, SC
Contact: 843-889-5842

Festivals and Events

Carolina Lowcountry Tomato Festival

This June festival started in 2006 and features a tomato cooking contest, a tomato growing contest, a street dance and more.
Location: Edisto Island, SC
Contact: Edisto Island Open Land Trust 843-869-7820

Useful Web Sites for Exploring the ACE Basin and Edisto Island

Charleston Area Convention and Visitors Bureau: www.charlestoncvb.com

Lowcountry/Resort Islands Tourism Commission: www.southcarolinalowcountry.com

SC Department of Natural Resources: www.dnr.sc.gov

Appendix

Additional Resources

Beasley, Barry and Tom Blagden. *The Rivers of South Carolina.* Englewood, Colorado: Westcliffe Publishers, 1999.

Boylston, Raymond P. *Healing Springs.* Orangeburg, SC: Sandlapper Publishing, 2004.

Bryan, Evelyn McDaniel Frazier. *Colleton County, S.C. A History of the First 160 Years 1670-1830.* Jacksonville, FL: The Florentine Press, 1993.

The Colleton County Historical Preservation Society and Nina Burke, *The Plantations of St. Bartholomew's Parish.* Paducah, KY: Turner Publishing Company, 2005.

Cooper, Jacquelyn Williams. *Springfield, South Carolina, A Small Town Saga in Orangeburg County.* Greenville, SC: A Press, 1988.

Culler, Daniel Marchant. *Orangeburgh District 1768-1868 History and Records.* Spartanburg, SC: The Reprint Co., Publishers, 1995.

Denton, James. "Where Old Soldiers Lie." *Sandlapper Magazine,* Summer, 2005.

Edgar, Walter. *South Carolina A History.* Columbia, SC: University of South Carolina Press, 1998.

Laurie, Pete. "Ageless Structures," *South Carolina Wildlife* (The South Carolina Department of Natural Resources), January-February 2006.

Linder, Suzanne Cameron, *Historical Atlas of the Rice Plantations of the ACE River Basin -1860,* The South Carolina Department of Archives and History, 1995.

McAmis, Herb, *Indian People of the Edisto River: A brief history of the Kusso-Natchez Indians often called "Edistos."* Colleton, SC: Four Holes Indian Organization.

Palmetto Conservation Foundation, *The Catawba River Companion.* Columbia, SC: PCF Press, 2003.

Peterson, Roger Tory, *Eastern Birds, A Field Guide to the Birds, Fourth Edition.* New York, NY: Houghton Mifflin Company, 1980.

Ramsay, David, *Edisto Island in 1808,* Edisto Island, SC: Edisto Island Historic Preservation Society, 1994.

Salley, A. S., *The History of Orangeburg County South Carolina: From Its First Settlement to the Close of the Revolutionary War.* Baltimore, MD: Regional Publishing Company, 1969.

South Carolina Department of Parks Recreation and Tourism, *Environmental Assessment of the South Carolina Heritage Corridor,* 2003.

South Carolina Educational Television, *Teachers Guide to South Carolina Geography,* 1041 George Rogers Boulevard, Columbia, SC.

South Carolina Water Resources Commission, *Assessing Change in the Edisto River Basin: An Ecological Characterization.* Columbia, SC: South Carolina Water Resources Commission, 1993.

Brochures and Guides

ACE Basin, The South Carolina Department of natural Resources, US Fish and Wildlife Service and the National Oceanic and Atmospheric Administration.

ACE Basin Current Events, South Carolina Department of Natural Resources, Summer 2003.

ACE Basin Current Events, South Carolina Department of Natural Resources, Fall 2004.

ACE Basin Current Events, South Carolina Department of Natural Resources, Winter 2005.

ACE Basin National Wildlife Refuge, US Fish and Wildlife Service.

Battleground of Freedom, Revolutionary War in South Carolina, South Carolina Department of Parks, Recreation and Tourism.

Birding the South Carolina Heritage Corridor, South Carolina Department of Parks, Recreation and Tourism.

Discover our Great Outdoors, Santee Country Tourism Region.

Edisto River Currents, Friends of the Edisto, Spring 2005.

The Francis Beidler Forest in Four Holes Swamp, A Self Guided Tour of the Boardwalk, National Audubon Society, 1978.

Garden Destinations, The South Carolina National Heritage Corridor.

Island Guide, The Official Guide of Edisto Island, Manna Publishing, North Charleston, SC, 2005-06.

National Wildlife Refuge System, A Visitors Guide, US Fish and Wildlife Service.

Old Jacksonborough Historic District, Colleton County Historical and Preservation Society.

Pon Pon Chapel of Ease of St. Bartholomew's Parish: Restoration Project, Colleton County Historic Preservation Society.

South Carolina Ducks at a Distance, Washington, DC, Outdoor Empire Publishing, 1978.

South Carolina Lowcountry Guidebook, Lowcountry Tourism Commission.

Visitors Guide, Thoroughbred County, Lower Savannah Council of Governments.

Web Sites

Bamberg County Chamber of Commerce
www.bambergcountychamber.org

Beidler Forest
www.beidlerforest.com

Carolina Home and Garden
www.carolinahomeandgarden.org

Charleston Area Convention and Visitors Bureau www.charlestoncvb.com

City of Aiken
www.aiken.net

City of Walterboro
www.walterborosc.org

Colleton County Chamber of Commerce
www.colletoncounty.org

Edisto Island Serpentarium
www.edistoserpentarium.com

Edisto River Canoe and Kayak Trail
www.edistoriver.org

Friends of the Edisto
www.edistofriends.org

Hitchcock Woods Foundation
www.hitchcockwoods.org

Lake Murray Tourism & Recreation Assoc.
www.lakemurraycountry.com

Lowcountry & Resort Islands Tourism Com.
www.southcarolinalowcountry.com

National Wild Turkey Center and Museum
www.nwtf.org

Orangeburg, SC Chamber of Commerce
www.orangeburgsc.net

Santee Cooper Counties Promotion Com.
www.santeecoopercountry.org

South Carolina Artisans Center
www.southcarolinaartisanscenter.org

South Carolina Bed & Breakfast Assoc.
www.southcarolinabedandbreakfast.com

South Carolina Campground Owners Assoc.
www.sccamping.com

South Carolina Department of Agriculture
www.state.sc.us/scda

South Carolina Dept. of Natural Resources
www.dnr.sc.gov

South Carolina Department of Parks,
Recreation and Tourism
www.discoversouthcarolina.com

South Carolina Heritage Corridor
www.sc-heritagecorridor.org

South Carolina Nature-Based Tourism Assoc.
http://scnatureadventures.com

South Carolina Peanut Party
www.scpeanutparty.com

South Carolina State Parks
www.southcarolinaparks.com

South Carolina State Trails program
www.SCtrails.net

Thoroughbred Country Tourism Region
www.tbredcountry.org

Paddling Trips on the Edisto

Adventure Carolina,
Cayce, SC 803-796-4505

Aiken State Natural Area,
Windsor, SC 803-649-2857

Beaufort Kayak Tours,
Beaufort, SC 843-525-0810

Blackwater Adventures,
Pinopolis, SC 843-761-1850

Carolina Heritage Outfitters,
Canadys, SC 29433 843-563-5051

Colleton State Park,
Canadys, SC 843-538-8206

Edisto River Canoe & Kayak Trail Com.
Walterboro, SC 843-549-5591

Givhans Ferry,
Ridgeville, SC 843-873-0692

Kayak Farm,
St. Helena Island, SC 29920
843-838-2008

About PCF Press

P CF Press is the publishing imprint of Palmetto Conservation Foundation. Our publications promote access and appreciation for South Carolina's natural and historic wonders. For inquiries or to order books, visit your local bookseller or our website at www.palmettoconservation.org.

Also from PCF PRESS...

The Waterfalls of South Carolina, Third Edition.
This unique guide is an essential exploring companion for every resident or visitor to South Carolina's spectacular mountains. Packed with stunning full-color photographs and easy to follow directions, this guide will take you to 31 waterfalls nestled in the rugged terrain of Greenville, Pickens and Oconee Counties.
88 pages, 32+ photographs, maps, and GPS waypoints. 6"x9" paperback.
ISBN 10: 0-974528-9-8 / ISBN 13: 978-0-9745284-9-6 $12.95

Favorite Family Hikes
The 30 walks compiled here represent a variety of trails and range of physical challenges, from strolls on the beach to mountainside scrambles. Geared toward trips for shorter legs (and attention spans) but anyone looking for a less strenuous —but still rewarding—getaway will enjoy this book, learn about wildlife, local history and neat destinations off the beaten path.
86 pages, detailed trail descriptions 6"x9" paperback
ISBN 10: 0-9745284-2-0 / ISBN 13: 9780974528427 $9.95

The Catawba River Companion
The only guidebook to the Catawba River in North and South Carolina. This book provides information on family getaways to popular destinations, maps and details on paddling trips, fishing and waterfall hikes, and recommendations for campgrounds or relaxing Bed & Breakfasts.
112 pages, maps, 6"x9", paperback
ISBN 0-9679016-8-5 / ISBN 13: 9780967901688 $9.95

Palmetto Trail Lowcountry Guide, Second Edition
The official guidebook to the Palmetto Trail from the Atlantic Coast to the Wateree River. Learn the history of the Lowcountry as well as find places to see, places to eat and places to stock up on supplies. Fifteen newly updated, detailed trail maps will guide you along some of South Carolina's most pristine natural scenery through 162 miles along the Palmetto Trail.
108 pages, 16 maps, 6" x 9", spiral bound
ISBN:0-9745284-7-1 / ISBN 13: 9780974528472 $17.95

About the Photographer

Bill Price is one of South Carolina's most experienced outdoor photographers. He has been exploring the South Carolina river regions for decades. He spent countless hours on and around the water of the Edisto to capture the images in *Edisto River Companion*. His work has also appeared in *South Carolina Wildlife*, *Sandlapper Magazine* and on several calendars. Price lives in Cassatt, SC, which is about 75 miles southeast of Rock Hill, SC. He also contributed to PCF Press's *The Catawba River Companion* and *Spider Lilies*.

Visit his website at www.billpricephotography.com.